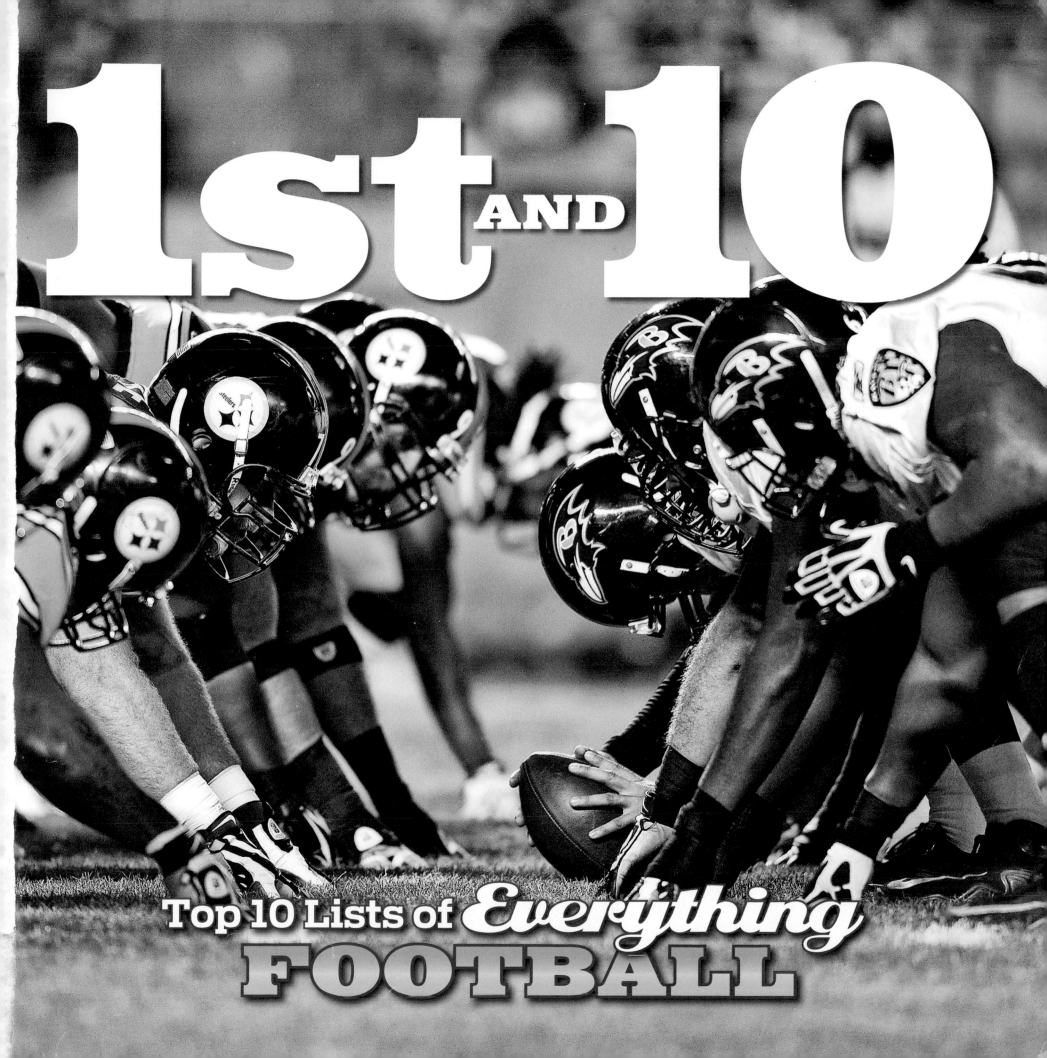

1st AND 10

Top 10 Lists of *Everything* FOOTBALL

Managing Editor, Sports Illustrated Kids **Mark Bechtel**

Creative Director **Beth Bugler**

Project Editor **Andrea Woo**

Director of Photography **Marguerite Schropp Lucarelli**

Photo Editors **Annmarie Avila, Linda Bonenfant**

Writers **Gary Gramling, Christina M. Tapper, Paul Ulane**

Editors **Justin Tejada, Sachin Shenolikar**

Copy Editor **Megan Collins**

Designer **Kirsten Sorton**

Premedia **Geoffrey Michaud, Dan Larkin, Robert Thompson**

Published by Liberty Street, an imprint of Time Inc. Books
225 Liberty Street
New York, New York 10281

LIBERTY STREET and SPORTS ILLUSTRATED KIDS are trademarks of Time Inc.

ISBN 10: 1-61893-173-3
ISBN 13: 978-1-61893-173-3
Library of Congress Control Number: 2016930816

Second edition, 2016

1 TLF 16

1 3 5 7 9 8 6 4 2

Time Inc. Books products may be purchased for business or promotional use. For information on bulk purchases, please contact
Christi Crowley in the Special Sales Department at (845) 895-9858.

We welcome your comments and suggestions about Time Inc. Books.
Please write to us at:
Time Inc. Books
Attention: Book Editors
P.O. Box 62310
Tampa, Florida 33662-2310

timeincbooks.com

Tom Brady is one of only three quarterbacks to win four Super Bowl titles.

The Top 10 Lists

Wide receiver Jo×nie Morton celebrates a touchdown by doing the Worm.

Chicago Bears–Green Bay Packers

No two teams have faced each other more often than the Bears and the Packers. The teams, whose home stadiums are only 200 miles apart, have played a whopping 190 games against each other through 2015. (The Bears have the edge, 93–91–6.) Those games have featured some of the best players in NFL history. The Bears have had 27 Hall of Famers who primarily played with Chicago, the most of any franchise. The Packers are second with 22 players in the Hall of Fame.

1

TOP 10
RIVAI

2 Dallas Cowboys–Washington Redskins

Greatness has defined this rivalry. These NFC East foes have 35 division titles and 10 NFL championships between them, including eight Super Bowls. Since the Cowboys entered the league as an expansion team in 1960, Dallas has had a major edge in its regular-season games against the Skins (65–41–2). But in the two times the teams met in the playoffs, Washington won both games.

3 Indianapolis Colts–New England Patriots

It's rare for a team to have a rival outside its division, but when each team has one of the best quarterbacks of all time — the Colts' Peyton Manning and Andrew Luck, and the Pats' Tom Brady — things are bound to get heated. When New England won the Super Bowl in 2003, '04, and '14, it had to get through the Colts in the postseason to get there. The opposite was true when Indianapolis won it all in 2007.

4 New York Giants–Philadelphia Eagles

These teams often face each other with an NFC East title on the line. The Giants may hold the overall edge (82–76–2) in regular-season matchups, but they've also suffered two of their most crushing defeats at the hands of the Eagles. In 1978, the Eagles returned a fumble for a touchdown with 20 seconds left to win the game in what became known as "The Miracle at the Meadowlands." In 2010, the G-Men took a 21-point lead into the fourth quarter, only to see Philly quarterback Michael Vick lead the Eagles on a stunning comeback that ended with DeSean Jackson's game-winning punt return for a touchdown as time expired.

5 Baltimore Ravens–Pittsburgh Steelers

With stars such as Baltimore's Ray Lewis and Ed Reed and Pittsburgh's James Harrison and Troy Polamalu, the Ravens and Steelers have had two of the best and hardest-hitting defenses in the game. Between 2008 and 2010, the Ravens and Steelers played seven games, including two in the playoffs. Only once was a game decided by more than a touchdown, and only once did a team score more than 23 points.

6 Green Bay Packers–Minnesota Vikings

These teams have some of the greatest legends in NFL history (such as Packers coach Vince Lombardi and Minnesota quarterback Fran Tarkenton). But the rivalry reached new heights when, in 2009, Packers legend Brett Favre joined the Purple People Eaters. Favre's games against his old team were some of the most-watched regular-season contests in NFL history.

7 Dallas Cowboys– San Francisco 49ers

The Niners and Cowboys don't meet often, but when they do, there's usually a lot on the line. Of their 34 matchups, six have been in the NFC Championship Game. Their 1982 battle included one of the most famous plays in sports history: the Catch. Trailing by six, San Francisco had a third down at the Dallas six-yard line with less than a minute left. Niners quarterback Joe Montana rolled right and threw toward wide receiver Dwight Clark in the back of the end zone. The pass was high because of the Cowboys' pressure, but Clark pulled it in, sending San Francisco to its first Super Bowl.

9 **Kansas City Chiefs–Oakland Raiders**
These division foes have a combined seven NFL and AFL titles, including four Super Bowls. One team has often stood in the other's way in the playoffs. As former Chiefs coach Hank Stram said, "We knew we had to go through Oakland to win the championship, and they knew they had to go through Kansas City."

8 **Miami Dolphins–New York Jets**
A lead is never safe when the Dolphins and Jets play. In 1994, Miami QB Dan Marino pretended to spike the ball before throwing a touchdown pass to cap a fourth-quarter comeback. In 2000, the Jets returned the favor with a 23-point come-from-behind win over the Dolphins on *Monday Night Football*.

10 **Denver Broncos–San Diego Chargers**
This surf-and-turf rivalry stretches from San Diego's beaches to Denver's mountains. The AFC West rivals have featured some powerful offenses over the years, led by such great quarterbacks as San Diego's Dan Fouts and Philip Rivers and Denver's John Elway and Peyton Manning.

Top
Qua

1 Joe Montana
San Francisco 49ers (1979–92), Kansas City Chiefs (1993–94)

Why is Joe Montana the greatest quarterback of all time? The Hall of Famer fueled a dynasty in San Francisco, leading the 49ers to four Super Bowl titles and winning the MVP award in three of those championships. Nobody was better in the clutch than Joe Cool. With the 49ers trailing the Cincinnati Bengals in Super Bowl XXIII, he led his team on a 92-yard drive that was capped off by a game-winning touchdown pass. The game was just one of the 31 late come-from-behind victories in his career. During his 15 pro seasons Montana had stellar stats: 40,551 passing yards, 273 touchdowns, and a 92.3 passer rating. His playoff numbers are just as impressive: Montana threw for 300 or more yards six times in the playoffs, and he had a 127.8 career passer rating in the Super Bowl. Most importantly, the 49ers were 16–7 in the playoffs with Montana under center.

10
arterbacks

2 Tom Brady
New England Patriots
(2000–present)

Growing up in Northern California, Tom Brady idolized 49ers legend Joe Montana. Twenty-five years after Montana's last Super Bowl victory, Brady finally matched his hero. When the Patriots superstar lifted the Lombardi Trophy after defeating the Seattle Seahawks in Super Bowl XLIX, Brady joined Montana and Terry Bradshaw as the only quarterbacks to win four Super Bowl titles. (In that game, Brady also became the first quarterback to appear in six Super Bowls.) If there's one thing Brady knows how to do, it's connect. His streak of 358 pass attempts without an interception during the 2010 and '11 seasons is an NFL record. He is one of two QBs to throw 50 touchdown passes in a season. He did that in 2007 while leading New England to the first 16–0 regular season in NFL history. Pretty impressive for a guy chosen with the 199th pick in the 2000 NFL Draft.

3 Johnny Unitas
Baltimore Colts (1956–72),
San Diego Chargers (1973)

Johnny Unitas's stats won't jump out at you. He completed only 54.6 percent of his passes and never had more than 3,500 yards in a season. But during Unitas's era, passing was much more difficult. With no defensive holding penalty, defenders were allowed to grab receivers until the ball arrived. When Johnny U. retired, he was the NFL's all-time leader in passing yards (40,239) and touchdown passes (290). He was a quarterback ahead of his time. He led the Colts to three league titles and was the first QB to perfect the two-minute offense, using it to win the 1958 NFL title game, one of the greatest football games ever played.

4 John Elway
Denver Broncos (1983–98)

If the Broncos were down, it wasn't wise to count them out, especially with John Elway under center. Elway directed 35 come-from-behind victories in the fourth quarter, including four in the playoffs. The Hall of Famer and nine-time Pro Bowler threw for 300 touchdowns and 51,475 yards during his 15 seasons in the league. His powerful arm wasn't the only threat to opponents: Elway rushed for 3,407 yards and 33 TDs. He is the only player in NFL history to pass for more than 3,000 yards and rush for more than 200 yards in seven straight seasons. Denver went to the Super Bowl five times behind Elway, winning twice.

5 Dan Marino
Miami Dolphins (1983–99)

Dan Marino, a one-man army during his time in Miami, might be the greatest athlete in sports to have never won a championship. Marino relied on his arm strength and quick release to make up for Miami's lack of a running game. His 61,361 career passing yards and 420 touchdowns both rank top-five all-time. In 1984, he threw for 5,084 passing yards, a single-season record that stood for 27 years, and 48 TDs, the fourth most all-time. Marino carried the Dolphins all the way to Super Bowl XIX. They lost that day, and Marino never made it back to the big game. Still, he's proof that there can be greatness beyond Super Bowl titles.

6 Peyton Manning
Indianapolis Colts (1998–2011),
Denver Broncos (2012–present)

The sign of a great QB is that he makes his team better. And man, has Peyton Manning made his teams better. Indianapolis had the league's worst record in 1997 and drafted Manning first overall the following year. He took the Colts to the playoffs in 11 of the next 13 seasons and led the team to victory in Super Bowl XLI. The Broncos went five straight years without a winning record before Manning joined them in 2012; they had at least 12 wins in each of his first three seasons in Denver, and they won Super Bowl 50. In 2013, Manning threw for 5,477 yards and 55 TDs, both single-season records, and won MVP for a record fifth time.

7 Brett Favre
Atlanta Falcons (1991),
Green Bay Packers (1992–2007),
New York Jets (2008),
Minnesota Vikings (2009–10)

Brett Favre took a lot of risks on the field, but when they paid off, they paid off in a big way. He won three consecutive MVP awards with the Green Bay Packers (1995–97) and led the Pack to victory in Super Bowl XXXI. Favre retired from the Packers in 2008 but returned, first with the Jets and then with the Vikings. In 2009, he had a career-high passer rating (107.2) and led Minnesota to the NFC Championship Game. Favre retired in 2010 as the NFL's all-time leader in passing yards (71,838), completions (6,300), and touchdowns (508).

8 Steve Young
Tampa Bay Buccaneers (1985–86),
San Francisco 49ers (1987–99)

Steve Young had to wait a long time for his chance, but when it came, he made the most of it. After a brief stint in the United States Football League and then two tough years with the Tampa Bay Buccaneers, Young spent four seasons as the backup to Joe Montana in San Francisco. Young finally became the starter in 1991 and showed that he could succeed on the big stage as well. In Super Bowl XXIX, Young threw a record six touchdown passes to lead the Niners to their fifth title. A lefty with great accuracy, Young won two NFL MVP awards and retired with the highest career passer rating of any QB with at least 10 seasons played (96.8).

9 Aaron Rodgers
Green Bay Packers
(2005–present)

Aaron Rodgers had big shoes to fill. He spent his first three NFL seasons backing up Brett Favre in Green Bay. When Favre changed his mind about retirement just before the 2008 season, many Packers fans wanted Favre back. But the Packers had already decided to pass the torch to Rodgers, who proceeded to torch opposing defenses with his passing. Rodgers made the Pro Bowl in his second season as a starter, and went on to win NFL MVP honors twice (2011 and '14). His on-point passing carried the Packers to victory in Super Bowl XLV. As of the end of the 2015 season, he had the highest career passer rating in NFL history (104.1).

10 Bart Starr
Green Bay Packers
(1956–71)

Bart Starr was used sparingly early in his career until legendary coach Vince Lombardi took over the Packers and turned Starr into a star. Starr's precise passing was a major reason for their success. He led the league in passing three times, and most importantly, he was at his best in the biggest games. He had a 9–1 career playoff record, is the only QB to win five NFL titles, and was MVP of Super Bowls I and II. Plus, Starr engineered arguably the greatest drive of all time: In the 1967 championship game against Dallas, he led a 68-yard, come-from-behind TD drive, completing all five of his passes and then diving in for the winning score.

Top 10 Team Name Backstories

1 Baltimore Ravens

Watching the skilled Baltimore Ravens defense attack can be like watching poetry in motion. That should come as no surprise since the team's nickname was inspired by a poet. Edgar Allan Poe, one of the greatest American writers, spent most of his adult life living in Baltimore, Maryland. While there in the 1830s, he is believed to have written his most famous poem, titled *The Raven*. When the Cleveland Browns moved to Baltimore before the 1996 season, the team's owners let fans vote on a new nickname, and Ravens won. The 2000 and '12 Super Bowl champs also have three mascots that look like the bird and are appropriately named Edgar, Allan, and Poe.

2 Chicago Bears

When founder and star player George Halas established the team in 1920, it was called the Staleys. In 1922, Halas wanted to rename the squad. Chicago's baseball team was the Cubs, and because football players are so much bigger than baseball players, Halas thought it made sense to call his team the Bears. The Bears went on to win nine championships, while the Cubs haven't won a World Series since 1908.

3 San Francisco 49ers

In 1848, the population of San Francisco, California, was about 800. After news spread that gold had been discovered in the area, thousands flocked to the city in 1849. Those pioneers inspired the name for the city's All-America Football Conference team, founded in 1946. Since then, the Niners have struck gold themselves, winning five Super Bowl titles.

4 New York Giants

In the 1920s, baseball was the most popular sport in the country. So when New York's first football team took the field in 1925, it took the name of one of the city's baseball teams. The baseball Giants moved to San Francisco after the 1957 season. The football Giants went on to win four Super Bowls.

5 Minnesota Vikings

Because many Minnesotans have roots in Scandinavian countries, general manager Bert Rose named the football team the Vikings in 1961, after the Nordic pirates who ruled the seas hundreds of years earlier. With their horn-painted helmets, the Vikings have made 27 playoff appearances.

6 Green Bay Packers

Curly Lambeau founded Green Bay's football team in 1919 while working for the Indian Packing Company, a meat-packing business. He persuaded his boss to donate $500 to the team and named it the Packers in honor of the sponsor. Even as the Packers became one of the most successful NFL teams, it never strayed from those local roots.

7 Philadelphia Eagles

The Eagles were founded in 1933 during the Great Depression. President Franklin D. Roosevelt had introduced the New Deal, a series of programs aimed at helping the country recover, and used an eagle as its symbol. Philly's football team adopted the bird as its own, and the three-time NFL champs have lifted the spirits of their fans ever since.

8 Buffalo Bills

The original Buffalo Bills played in the All-America Football Conference. The team name was inspired by the famous frontiersman Buffalo Bill Cody. That team folded in 1949, but when Buffalo became a charter member of the AFL in 1960, it adopted the name of its former pro team. The Bills are still the only team to play in four consecutive Super Bowls.

9 Cleveland Browns

The Browns are the only team named after a football personality, Paul Brown, the team's first coach and general manager. Fans voted for the name in 1945, even though Brown was not in favor of it. But the fans chose wisely: Brown went on to lead Cleveland to seven league championships.

10 Tennessee Titans

After the Houston Oilers moved to Tennessee in 1997, they were simply the Tennessee Oilers. In 1999, the team decided to change its name to the Titans because it reflected "strength, leadership, and other heroic qualities." That season they reached the first Super Bowl in team history.

1 West Coast Offense

The San Francisco 49ers made this system famous in the 1980s and '90s. Created by Hall of Fame head coach Bill Walsh and executed by Hall of Fame quarterback Joe Montana, the West Coast offense relies on a series of short passes intended to free up receivers for long runs after the catch. Between Walsh and Montana, and later head coach George Seifert and quarterback Steve Young, the Niners won five Super Bowls with the system. Variations of the West Coast offense are still in heavy use in the NFL today.

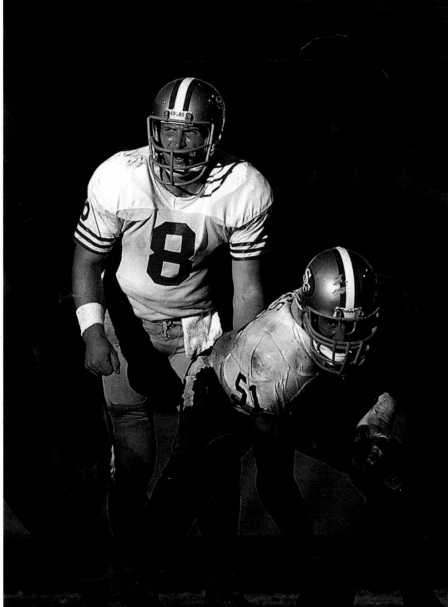

2 3–4 Defense

Former University of Oklahoma coach Chuck Fairbanks brought the 3–4 defense with him when he became head coach of the New England Patriots in the mid-1970s. The formation features three linemen at the line of scrimmage, with four linebackers behind them. Linebackers play a big role as pass rushers in the 3–4, often geting more sacks than the linemen.

3 Tampa 2 Defense

Tampa Bay Buccaneers head coach Tony Dungy and defensive coordinator Monte Kiffin popularized this defensive scheme in the mid-1990s. The Tampa 2 is effective at preventing big plays because two safeties and the middle linebacker drop back deep into coverage. The outside linebackers and cornerbacks cover shorter routes. Pressure from the four defensive linemen is essential to the Tampa 2.

4 T Formation

Chicago Bears owner-coach George Halas brought this formation to pro football in the 1940s. Three running backs line up behind the quarterback, who's directly under center, in the shape of the letter T. It was was the first formation that allowed the quarterback to take the snap directly under center before either handing off the ball or passing downfield to a receiver. It's the basis for almost all standard offensive plays in the game today.

5 Spread Offense

Warren Moon and the Houston Oilers popularized the original version of this scheme, which spreads out the offensive players — using either one or no running back — to force the defense to spread out too. If the field is properly spaced, the spread offense will weaken the opposing pass rush.

6 Nickel Defense

In the mid-1950s, the Philadelphia Eagles' Chicago Special defense used an extra defensive back to cover Hall of Fame tight end Mike Ditka. Formations employing a fifth defensive back, who is meant to help neutralize big plays in the passing game, later became known as the nickel.

7 46 Defense

Buddy Ryan created this scheme as defensive coordinator of the Chicago Bears in the 1980s. The 46 puts more players near the line of scrimmage so that offensive players are unsure of who to block. In 1985, the 46 defense helped the Bears go 15–1 and win the Super Bowl.

8 Run and Shoot

The Atlanta Falcons and Detroit Lions introduced this improvisational scheme to the NFL in 1990. The offense is based on sending receivers in motion before the snap to set up mismatches and reveal defensive coverages.

9 Air Coryell

In the late 1970s and early 1980s, San Diego Chargers head coach Don Coryell electrified the football world by emphasizing the deep pass on offense. Coryell's Chargers led the league in passing yards for six straight seasons, from 1978 through '83.

10 Read-Option

Popularized by quarterbacks like Russell Wilson and Colin Kaepernick, the read-option took the NFL by storm around 2012. The quarterback takes a shotgun snap and either hands to the running back or keeps the ball and runs it himself, depending on what he "reads" a defensive lineman is doing on the play. However, many teams have shied away from the read-option for fear of their quarterback taking too many hits.

Top 10 Play Innovations

① Refrigerator

William Perry,
Defensive Tackle

When William Perry's friend at Clemson told him he looked like a walking refrigerator, he had found the perfect nickname. At 6'2" and 335 pounds, the defensive tackle was a larger-than-life player. In addition to clogging the middle of the field on defense, Perry sometimes played fullback, clearing the way for Hall of Fame running back Walter Payton. Perry even carried the ball on occasion, scoring a touchdown in the Chicago Bears' 1985 Super Bowl win. Perry's prize for that Super Bowl victory was a size-25 championship ring, more than double the average man's ring size. In 10 NFL seasons with the Bears and the Philadelphia Eagles, the Fridge had 29.5 sacks and scored three touchdowns.

② Bus

Jerome Bettis
Running Back

Jerome Bettis was known for going the distance with multiple defenders on his back, which is why his college newspaper named him Bus. Bettis took plenty of defenders to school during his 13 NFL seasons with the Los Angeles/St. Louis Rams and the Pittsburgh Steelers. In 2015, Bus made one final stop: He was inducted into the Pro Football Hall of Fame.

③ Crazy Legs

Elroy Hirsch
Halfback-End

Hall of Famer Elroy Hirsch earned his nickname when he zipped past defenders for a 61-yard touchdown while playing for the University of Wisconsin in 1942. He kept his wild style of running after turning pro and helped the Los Angeles Rams win the 1951 NFL title.

Top 10 Nickna

④ Prime Time

Deion Sanders *Cornerback*

With an outspoken personality and high-stepping celebrations in the end zone, Deion Sanders was as entertaining as he was talented. The two-time Super Bowl champion first earned his nickname in high school. He continued to attract attention in college and the pros, so the name stuck. Sanders maximized his exposure, playing 13 seasons in the NFL and nine seasons in Major League Baseball.

⑤ Sweetness

Walter Payton *Running Back*

Walter Payton's label was a nod to the nine-time Pro Bowler's pleasant personality and his nimble running style. The Hall of Famer was the heart and soul of the Chicago Bears for 13 seasons, rushing for 16,726 yards and 110 touchdowns.

⑥ Night Train

Dick Lane *Defensive Back*

Named after the 1952 hit song *Night Train*, Dick Lane was one of the most feared tacklers in the NFL. Wide receivers did not want to see Lane barreling down the tracks in their direction. His 14 interceptions as a rookie in 1952 remains an NFL record.

⑦ Broadway Joe

Joe Namath *Quarterback*

Teammate Sherman Plunkett gave Joe Namath his nickname after the New York Jets QB appeared on a 1965 SPORTS ILLUSTRATED cover with New York's iconic Broadway as its backdrop. Namath was known for his bold statements. He famously guaranteed a win over the Baltimore Colts in Super Bowl III and delivered.

⑧ Megatron
Calvin Johnson *Wide Receiver*

At 6' 5" and 235 pounds, Calvin Johnson is one the biggest receivers ever. And with a 40-yard dash time of 4.35, he's one of the fastest. He's so good it often seems like he's from another planet. So, fittingly, teammate Roy Williams named Johnson after one of the most powerful Transformers.

⑨ Mean Joe Greene
Joe Greene *Defensive Tackle*

Rarely did you see the Hall of Famer's name without his nickname in front of it. Mean Joe Greene, who had played for the North Texas State Mean Green, was a dominant force during the Pittsburgh Steelers' Steel Curtain era. He helped the squad win four Super Bowls in the 1970s.

⑩ Joe Cool
Joe Montana *Quarterback*

Joe Montana lived up to his nickname by staying calm under pressure. A four-time Super Bowl winner and three-time Super Bowl MVP with the San Francisco 49ers, Montana was cool as a cucumber while passing for 40,551 yards and 273 touchdowns in 15 NFL seasons.

Top 10 Helmets

1 Cincinnati Bengals

The orange-and-black stripes on the players' helmets make them look like jungle cats stalking their prey. When the team debuted in 1968, its helmet was all orange with the word BENGALS in block letters on the side. In 1981, Cincinnati removed the team name and added the signature stripes, which matched purr-fectly with the Bengals' uniforms. Coincidentally, the same season the Bengals changed their helmet, they went to the Super Bowl.

2 **St. Louis Rams**
Other than tweaks in color, the golden horns designed by Rams halfback Fred Gehrke have remained the same since 1948.

3 **Pittsburgh Steelers**
Pittsburgh is the only team to have its logo — a nod to the American Iron and Steel Institute — on just one side of the helmet.

4 **San Diego Chargers**
Lightning first struck the Chargers' headgear in 1960, but the bolt has changed colors five times since then.

5 **New England Patriots**
For 32 years, mascot Pat Patriot was shown snapping the ball on the helmet. Flying Elvis made his debut in 1993.

6 **Chicago Bears**
The iconic C first appeared on the helmet in 1962. In 1973 the letter changed from white to orange.

7 **Dallas Cowboys**
The single blue-and-white star is symbolic of Texas, also known as the Lone Star State.

8 **Denver Broncos**
Giddyup! Denver's helmet has undergone numerous logo changes since the 1960s. In 1997, the team settled on the wild horse.

9 **San Francisco 49ers**
The Niners brightened things up for the 2009 season, reverting from a cardinal red logo to the team's original cherry red.

10 **Green Bay Packers**
Interestingly, cheeseheads didn't always wear green. Blue and yellow were the Packers' colors until 1950.

Top 10 Touchdown Leaders

1

Jerry Rice

Career Touchdowns: 208

Using power, speed, and athleticism, wide receiver Jerry Rice blazed past defenses and tore through the record book during his 20 seasons (1985–2004) in the NFL. Rice tops the all-time lists for touchdowns, receptions (1,549), and receiving yards (22,895). Rice also had a record number of 1,000-yard receiving seasons (14). The Hall of Famer, who spent 16 seasons with the San Francisco 49ers, propelled the team to three Super Bowl victories and was named MVP of Super Bowl XXIII. Part of what made Rice so amazing was that he was so good for so long. At 40 years old, he helped the Oakland Raiders reach Super Bowl XXXVII against the Tampa Bay Buccaneers. He had five receptions, 77 yards, and one touchdown in the Raiders' loss.

2 **Emmitt Smith**
Career TDs: **175**
Critics said Emmitt Smith was too small to star in the NFL. But that didn't stop the 5'9", 216-pound running back from becoming one of the best players in league history. Smith is the all-time leader in career rushing yards (18,355) and rushing TDs (164). The NFL and Super Bowl MVP of the 1993 season, Smith finished with five career rushing touchdowns in title games, also an NFL record.

3 **LaDainian Tomlinson**
Career TDs: **162**
In 2009 running back LaDainian Tomlinson scored his 150th touchdown in just his 137th game. No other player reached the milestone faster. A five-time Pro Bowler, Tomlinson won the NFL MVP award in 2006, when he set the single-season touchdown record (31). He joined the New York Jets in 2010 after scoring 153 touchdowns in just nine seasons for the Chargers.

4 **Randy Moss**
Career TDs: **157**
Known for his stunning catches, the tall (6'4") and agile Moss is one of the top receiving threats ever to pull on a helmet. The wideout set the single-season record for touchdown catches by a rookie in 1998 (17) and followed it up by setting the overall record in 2007 (23).

5 **Terrell Owens**
Career TDs: **156**
Terrell Owens is as famous for his celebrations in the end zone as he is for his ability to get there. But the wideout is not all flash. While playing for the Philadelphia Eagles in 2004, he showed his toughness, returning to play in Super Bowl XXXIX despite having broken his right leg in Week 15. Owens finished the game with 122 receiving yards in the Eagles' loss. Over a 15-year career with five NFL teams, Owens caught 1,078 passes.

6 **Marcus Allen**
Career TDs: **145**
With a graceful running style, Marcus Allen was the first player in league history to pile up more than 10,000 rushing yards and 5,000 receiving yards. The Hall of Fame running back earned Rookie of the Year (1982), MVP (1985), and Super Bowl MVP (1983) honors while playing for the Los Angeles Raiders before finishing his career with the Kansas City Chiefs. A master of short-yardage and goal-line situations, Allen played in six Pro Bowls.

7 **Marshall Faulk**
Career TDs: **136**
During his 13 seasons with the Indianapolis Colts and St. Louis Rams, Marshall Faulk was one of the most versatile running backs in the league. In 1999 he became the second player in NFL history to have at least 1,000 yards rushing and receiving. Faulk scored three touchdowns in his first NFL game, in 1994, and never looked back. During his MVP season in 2000, he scored 26 TDs (a single-season record at the time). Faulk was elected to the Hall of Fame in 2011.

8 **Cris Carter**
Career TDs: **131**
Wide receiver Cris Carter was known for his spectacular footwork and great hands. While playing for the Minnesota Vikings in 2000, he became only the second player in NFL history to reach 1,000 receptions. He had a league-leading 17 touchdowns in 1995, as well as back-to-back 122-catch seasons in 1994 and '95. Carter, who also suited up for the Philadelphia Eagles and Miami Dolphins, is the Vikings' all-time leader in touchdowns (110) and receptions (1,004).

9 **Marvin Harrison**
Career TDs: **128**
A staple of the Indianapolis Colts' offense from 1996 through 2008, Marvin Harrison was the first player in NFL history to have eight straight seasons with 10 or more touchdown receptions. The wide receiver made an immediate impact with his nifty catches and consistency. Harrison's streak of 190 consecutive games with a catch is the longest to begin an NFL career.

10 **Jim Brown**
Career TDs: **126**
Until 2006, no player reached the 100-touchdown mark faster than three-time NFL MVP Jim Brown (who did it in 1964 after 93 games). Brown even threw three career TD passes. But the fullback shined brightest carrying the ball: He cut through defenses with power and agility and was the NFL's rushing leader in eight of his nine seasons with the Cleveland Browns.

Top 10 PRO FOOTBALL MOVIES

DELICIOUS NUTRITIOUS

BASED ON THE EXTRAORDINARY TRUE STORY

SANDRA BULLOCK
THE BLIND SIDE

NOVEMBER 20

The Blind Side

1 The story of NFL offensive tackle Michael Oher is movingly told in this film. Oher was a homeless teenager when he met Leigh Anne and Sean Tuohy (Sandra Bullock and Tim McGraw). The family adopted Oher and paved the way for him to attend the University of Mississippi, where he became a star. Bullock won an Oscar for her performance as the strong-willed mom.

IF YOU CAN'T GET OUT
GET EVEN

ADAM SANDLER CHRIS ROCK
THE LONGEST YARD

IT'S TIME TO EVEN THE SCORE
MEMORIAL DAY 2005

6 The Longest Yard

Adam Sandler plays Paul Crewe, a former pro QB who lands in prison and gets thrown into a game between the inmates and the guards. A few of the recognizable faces in this comedy: Hall of Famer Michael Irvin and SPORTS ILLUSTRATED writer Peter King.

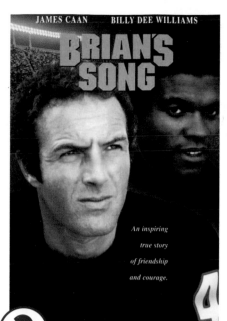

2 Brian's Song

Neither race nor disease could break the strong bond between the Bears' Gale Sayers (Billy Dee Williams) and Brian Piccolo (James Caan). The story takes a tragic turn when Piccolo is diagnosed with cancer. *Brian's Song* is a movie that values the importance of friendship, teammates, and courage.

3 Invincible

It's every fan's dream to play for his favorite team, and Vince Papale (Mark Wahlberg) does just that in *Invincible*. A substitute teacher, Papale attends an open tryout for the Philadelphia Eagles. He grabs coach Dick Vermeil's attention and goes on to become a special-teams standout for three years.

4 Paper Lion

It's not as easy as it looks to play quarterback in the NFL — just ask George Plimpton. Based on his real-life experience, Plimpton (Alan Alda) is a Sports Illustrated writer who tries out for quarterback during training camp with the Detroit Lions. The results are not pretty, but they are funny.

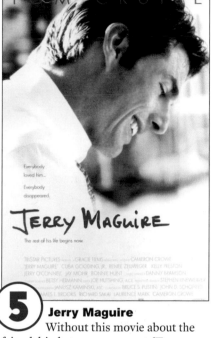

5 Jerry Maguire

Without this movie about the friendship between an agent (Tom Cruise) and his star player (Cuba Gooding Jr.), we wouldn't have the catchphrase "Show me the money!" Gooding won a best supporting actor Oscar for playing outspoken wide receiver Rod Tidwell.

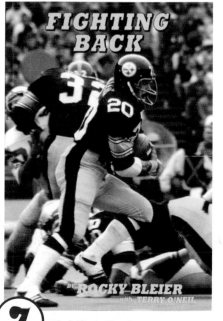

7 Fighting Back

Drafted to fight in the Vietnam War during his playing career, Rocky Bleier (Robert Urich) is injured in battle and comes home barely able to walk. Not only does he get back on his feet, Bleier returns to the Pittsburgh Steelers to help them win the Super Bowl.

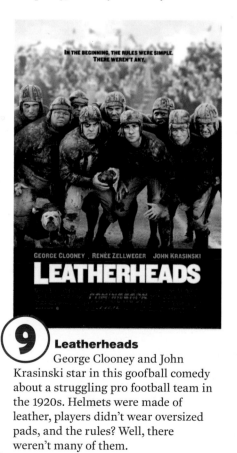

8 The Replacements

When the professional players go on strike, a head coach (Gene Hackman) is forced to take the field with a group of misfits. The initial results are disastrous, and hilarious. But the team rallies around its quarterback (Keanu Reeves) and comes together when it counts.

9 Leatherheads

George Clooney and John Krasinski star in this goofball comedy about a struggling pro football team in the 1920s. Helmets were made of leather, players didn't wear oversized pads, and the rules? Well, there weren't many of them.

10 The Game Plan

Dwayne Johnson plays Joe Kingman, a pro football superstar who learns he has an eight-year-old daughter (Madison Pettis). Kingman has to juggle his gridiron career with his new responsibilities as a dad, which include trips to ballet practice.

Top 10
Super
Bowls

Super Bowl XLII
February 3, 2008
New York Giants 17
New England Patriots 14

It was a massive mismatch on paper. The Patriots came into the game 18–0 with two-time Super Bowl MVP Tom Brady leading the highest-scoring offense in league history. The Giants were a wild card team that had finished the season 10–6. But once the game kicked off, it was clear the G-Men were not going to back down. New York used a fierce pass rush led by Justin Tuck to sack Brady five times and keep the game close. The score was 10–7 heading into the final quarter, when the lead changed hands three times. The game-winning score came at the end of a 12-play Giants drive that was kept alive by what will forever be known as the Helmet Catch. With 1:15 left in the game, facing third-and-five from his own 44-yard line, Giants quarterback Eli Manning dodged defenders to complete a 32-yard pass to receiver David Tyree. Tyree brought the ball down by trapping it against his helmet in heavy traffic. Four plays later, Manning found Plaxico Burress in the end zone as the Giants took the lead for good and ended the Patriots' dream of a perfect season.

2 Super Bowl III
January 12, 1969
New York Jets 16   Baltimore Colts 7

After being blown out in the first two Super Bowls, the American Football League was looking to make a big statement in the third championship game against the NFL. Joe Namath, of the AFL's Jets, did just that. In the week leading up to the game, the quarterback boldly made a public guarantee that the Jets would bring home the title for the AFL. Broadway Joe backed up his claim by leading New York to a shocking upset of the 15–1 Colts, earning the game's MVP honors in the process. The AFL's first championship-game victory remains one of the biggest upsets in Super Bowl history.

3 Super Bowl XXXIV

January 30, 2000

St. Louis Rams 23   Tennessee Titans 16

The Titans were one yard short of forcing the first overtime in Super Bowl history. Kurt Warner directed the Rams' offense, nicknamed the Greatest Show on Turf, up and down the field for 436 yards, but the Titans stormed back from a 16–0 deficit to tie the game with 2:12 on the clock. After a quick touchdown by the Rams, the Titans drove the ball to the Rams' 10-yard line with six seconds left. On the game's final play, Titans QB Steve McNair hit receiver Kevin Dyson, but Dyson was tackled at the one-yard line as the clock struck zero on the Titans' season.

4 Super Bowl XXV

January 27, 1991

New York Giants 20   Buffalo Bills 19

The Bills were averaging 47.5 points per game in the playoffs before they ran into the Giants and their ball-control offense. New York held the ball for more than 40 minutes of the game, keeping the Bills' powerful offense off the field for all but eight minutes in the second half. Still, the Bills trailed by only one point when they got the ball back at their own 10-yard line with 2:16 to play. Quarterback Jim Kelly led Buffalo down the field to the Giants' 29-yard line, setting up a 47-yard field goal attempt for kicker Scott Norwood with four seconds left. Norwood missed the kick wide right, setting off a string of four consecutive Super Bowl defeats for the Bills.

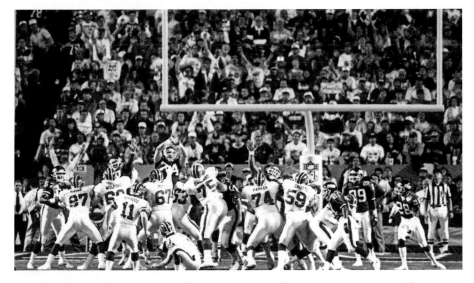

5 Super Bowl XLIII

February 1, 2009

Pittsburgh Steelers 27

Arizona Cardinals 23

The Cardinals' first-ever Super Bowl appearance wasn't a winning effort, but it was a thrilling one. The game produced three memorable moments: Pittsburgh linebacker James Harrison returning an interception 100 yards for a touchdown just before halftime, Arizona wideout Larry Fitzgerald racing 64 yards to give the Cardinals a 23–20 lead with 2:37 left in the game, and Steelers wide receiver Santonio Holmes snatching a TD pass in the corner of the end zone with 35 seconds left. Holmes's grab gave the Steelers an NFL-record sixth Super Bowl title.

6 ### Super Bowl XXIII

January 22, 1989 **San Francisco 49ers 20   Cincinnati Bengals 16**

Over his career, Joe Montana led 31 fourth-quarter comebacks. This Super Bowl victory was the most memorable. After a first half that ended tied 3–3, both offenses came alive in the second half, scoring a combined 30 points. With 3:20 left, the Niners were trailing by three and backed up on their own eight-yard line. Instead of immediately calling the play in the huddle, Montana pointed out actor John Candy in the stands to make sure his teammates were relaxed. The move worked. Montana completed eight of nine passes on the drive and hit receiver John Taylor with the 10-yard, game-winning TD pass with 34 seconds left. The win marked the Niners' third Super Bowl title of the 1980s.

7 ### Super Bowl XXXVI

February 3, 2002 **New England Patriots 20   St. Louis Rams 17**

Tom Brady started the 2001 season as a little-known backup and ended the year as the Super Bowl MVP after leading the Patriots to one of the biggest upsets in Super Bowl history. New England used a smart defensive game plan to slow down the high-flying Rams, that season's highest-scoring team. Then Brady and the Pats took over possession with less than two minutes remaining in the fourth quarter and the score tied 17–17. Starting at their own 17-yard line, the Patriots decided against running out the clock and playing for overtime. Instead, New England trusted Brady to lead the team down the field. And, boy, did he deliver. Brady drove the Pats to the St. Louis 30-yard line to set up Adam Vinatieri's game-winning, 48-yard field goal as time ran out.

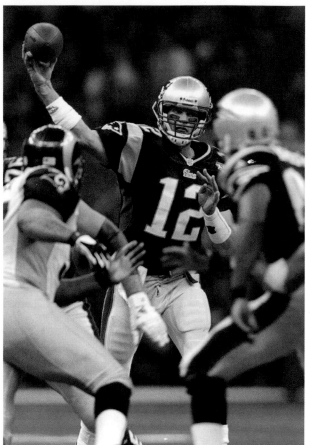

9 ### Super Bowl XXXVIII

February 1, 2004

New England Patriots 32 Carolina Panthers 29

Few Super Bowls had as much action packed into the final quarter as this one. The Panthers and the Patriots combined for 37 points and four ties or lead changes in the final period alone. A 33-yard TD run by Panthers running back DeShaun Foster and an 85-yard TD reception by the Panthers' Muhsin Muhammad helped Carolina keep pace with the Pats until Tom Brady worked his magic. With the score tied 29–29 late in the fourth quarter, Brady needed only 1:04 to march his team into field goal range, which paved the way for Adam Vinatieri to boot the game-winning 41-yarder with four seconds left on the clock.

8 Super Bowl XLIX

February 1, 2015

New England Patriots 28 Seattle Seahawks 24

Seattle had opened up a 10-point lead after three quarters, but the Patriots came storming back. Tom Brady led two long touchdown drives in the fourth quarter to give New England the lead. Then each team made an unforgettable play. Driving with a little more than a minute left, Seahawks QB Russell Wilson threw a long pass down the right sideline. It was tipped by cornerback Malcolm Butler, then bounced off receiver Jermaine Kearse's leg as he fell to the ground. Sitting down, Kearse reached out and grabbed it for a 33-yard gain to the five-yard line. Facing second-and-goal from the one-yard line, Seattle seemed sure to score the winning touchdown with star runner Marshawn Lynch lined up in the backfield. Instead they tried to throw a slant pass. Butler, an undrafted rookie who hadn't even started the game, jumped in and intercepted the throw. It was the most thrilling game-winning play in Super Bowl history.

10 Super Bowl X

January 18, 1976

Pittsburgh Steelers 21 Dallas Cowboys 17

Lynn Swann put his stamp on this contest with a pair of huge catches. The first took place in the second quarter, when Swann reeled in a 53-yard bomb from Steelers quarterback Terry Bradshaw with a juggling catch. Swann then snagged a 64-yard TD with three minutes left in the game. He finished with 161 receiving yards and won the game's MVP trophy. The Steelers, however, didn't clinch their second consecutive Super Bowl title until safety Glen Edwards intercepted a pass by Roger Staubach on the game's final play.

TOP 10 FAST

1 Chris Johnson
Running Back

There's speed on the track, and then there's speed on the field. Chris Johnson has both. CJ clocked the fastest 40-yard dash time in NFL combine history (4.24 seconds). He's also the only player in NFL history to have three touchdown runs of 85 yards or longer.

2 Deion Sanders
Cornerback

Deion Sanders returned a punt for a touchdown in his very first NFL game and never slowed down. In his 14-season career, he scored six TDs on punt returns, three on kickoff returns, and nine on interceptions. He even caught three TD passes on offense. Sanders was so fast, he often had enough time to high-step his way into the end zone.

3 Bob Hayes
Wide Receiver

In 1964, Bob Hayes earned the title of World's Fastest Man by winning gold in the 100 meters at the Tokyo Olympics. He didn't disappoint in the NFL, either. Bullet Bob shot onto the scene as a Cowboys rookie in 1965, leading the team with 1,003 receiving yards. The Hall of Famer still owns the Cowboys record for career touchdown receptions (71).

4 Bo Jackson
Running Back

Bo Jackson's old commercial featured the catchphrase "Bo knows football." Well, Bo knew speed, too. In three of his four NFL seasons, Jackson had a run of 88 yards or longer. He used his powerful running style to get past the initial line of defense, but after that, it was off to the races. And Bo usually won.

5 Darrell Green
Cornerback

This seven-time Pro Bowler never lost a step during his 20-year Hall of Fame career. Darrell Green won the NFL's Fastest Man competition four times and was one of the most feared cornerbacks ever. His ability to quickly close on the receiver helped him intercept a pass in 19 straight seasons, an NFL record. Green returned six of his 54 career picks for TDs.

ST PLAYERS

6 **Randy Moss**
Wide Receiver
One of the most dangerous deep threats, Randy Moss broke the single-season mark for most touchdown catches in a season (23) in 2007 and has had over 1,000 yards receiving in 10 of his 13 NFL seasons. His soft hands and blinding speed put him in a second-place tie for the most touchdown receptions in league history (153).

7 **Willie Gault**
Wide Receiver
Willie Gault was a member of the 4×100-meter relay team that set the world record at the 1983 world championships. That speed served Gault well when the Chicago Bears drafted him later that year. He averaged almost 20 yards per catch in the NFL and was the main deep threat for Chicago during its 1985 Super Bowl–winning season.

8 **Devin Hester**
Wide Receiver,
Kick Returner
Once Devin Hester gets a head of steam, look out. The first player in NFL history to return the opening kickoff of the Super Bowl for a touchdown, Hester needed only five seasons to set the league record for most kick-return TDs (14). His speed has made him one of the few special-teams players that is a threat to score whenever he touches the ball.

9 **Cliff Branch**
Wide Receiver
Cliff Branch's blazing speed helped him land on four Pro Bowl teams and three first-team All-Pro squads. The quick receiver led the league in touchdown catches twice and receiving yards once. Among wide receivers with at least 500 career catches, Branch ranks seventh all-time with an average of 17.3 yards per catch.

10 **Ron Brown**
Wide Receiver,
Kick Returner
After winning Olympic gold in the 4×100-meter relay at the 1984 Olympics in Los Angeles, Ron Brown decided to put on the pads, signing a four-year deal with the Los Angeles Rams. In 1985, his second season with L.A., Brown led the league in kickoff-return touchdowns and yards per kick return, earning an invite to the Pro Bowl.

Top 10

FANTASY
Performers

1 Marshall Faulk
Running Back, St. Louis Rams (2000)

Marshall Faulk didn't exactly take the fantasy football world by surprise in 2000. In 1999, the Hall of Famer became the second player in NFL history to finish a season with at least 1,000 yards rushing and receiving. The following season, Faulk piled up huge yardage again (1,359 rushing, 830 receiving). The stunning part was that his 26 touchdowns nearly doubled his previous career high. Despite missing two games in 2000, Faulk still averaged 29.7 fantasy points per game, an all-time record. If you had Faulk on your team in 2000, you were almost *guaranteed* a championship.

2 Priest Holmes *Running Back, Kansas City Chiefs (2002)*
Priest Holmes had a remarkable 2,287 yards from scrimmage and 24 TDs despite missing two games in 2002. The only problem: Those games he missed were the last two of the season, meaning he sat out a lot of fantasy championship games.

3 Peyton Manning *Quarterback, Denver Broncos (2013)*

In 2004, Peyton Manning broke Dan Marino's single-season touchdown-pass record of 48 by one. In '07, Tom Brady broke Manning's mark by one. When Manning re-set the record, he blew it away. Peyton tossed 55 TDs in '13, and also set the single-season passing yardage record (5,477). It was the greatest statistical season ever by a QB.

4 Tom Brady *Quarterback, New England Patriots (2007)*
After throwing for 3,529 yards and 24 touchdowns in 2006, Tom Brady was considered a solid but unspectacular fantasy QB. Then came 2007. Teaming up with new receivers Randy Moss and Wes Welker, Brady threw for 4,806 yards and became the first quarterback to ever throw 50 touchdowns in a season.

5 LaDainian Tomlinson *Running Back, San Diego Chargers (2006)*
LaDainian Tomlinson shattered the NFL single-season touchdown record with 31 in 2006, including six games in which he reached the end zone at least three times. The only thing keeping him from the top spot on this list: LT failed to score in the season's final two games, preventing many fantasy owners from winning their leagues.

6 Jerry Rice *Wide Receiver, San Francisco 49ers (1995)*
Fantasy football wasn't as popular in 1995 as it is today, but that was the year Jerry Rice had the greatest fantasy season ever by a wide receiver. His 1,848 receiving yards are second all-time, and only four receivers have topped Rice's 122 catches in '95. In Week 15 (playoffs for most fantasy leagues), Rice caught 14 passes for 289 yards and three TDs.

7 Daunte Culpepper *Quarterback, Minnesota Vikings (2004)*

Going into the 2004 season, Daunte Culpepper wasn't known for his passing. That changed when he threw for 4,717 yards and 39 touchdown passes that year. Culpepper didn't give his legs a rest either: He ran for an impressive 406 yards and two more TDs, making it one of the best fantasy seasons ever.

8 Randy Moss *Wide Receiver, New England Patriots (2007)*

After Randy Moss caught a career-low 42 passes for 553 yards with the Oakland Raiders in 2006, many thought he was washed up. They were wrong. Moss slipped to the middle rounds of fantasy drafts, but teaming up with Tom Brady, he caught an NFL-record 23 touchdowns and had 1,493 receiving yards.

9 Rob Gronkowski *Tight End, New England Patriots (2011)*
Normally, it's hard to find a productive tight end in fantasy football. But if you've ever had Gronk on your team, especially in 2011, you were in luck. In just his second NFL season, the Patriots star had more touchdown catches (17) and receiving yards (1,327) than any tight end in NFL history.

10 Baltimore Ravens *Defense (2000)*

The old saying "defense wins championships" doesn't usually apply to fantasy football, but having the Baltimore D in 2000 certainly helped. Led by Ray Lewis, the Ravens allowed only 10.3 points per game that season, the lowest in the NFL since 1977, and forced 49 turnovers.

Top 10
UNBREAKABLE Records

1 Otto Graham's 10 consecutive championship-game appearances

To get a sense of how impressive Otto Graham's streak is, consider that Tom Brady, Joe Montana, and Brett Favre have played in 12 championship games *combined*. Graham played in four straight championships in the All-America Football Conference and then six in the NFL. He was victorious in seven of the 10 title games.

2 Don Shula's 347 career coaching wins

Don Shula, who coached in the NFL from 1963 through '95, is in a league of his own. The active coach closest to Shula in the wins column through 2014: Bill Belichick, with 233 victories.

3 Tom Landry's 29 straight seasons coaching one team

Tom Landry took over a stumbling franchise and turned it into America's Team. Under Landry, the Dallas Cowboys won two Super Bowls. With the coaching carousel of today's game, it's unlikely we'll see that kind of longevity with one team again.

4 The Tampa Bay Buccaneers' 26 straight losses

After going 0–14 in their debut season, the Bucs kicked off their second season with a 12-game losing streak. John McKay, coach of the futile Bucs, once joked that the team couldn't stop the run or the pass — but otherwise it was in good shape.

5 The 1972 Miami Dolphins' undefeated season

In 1972, the Dolphins went unbeaten during the NFL's 14-game regular season and then won three more games in the playoffs, including the Super Bowl. The New England Patriots went into Super Bowl XLII with an 18–0 record but lost to the New York Giants in the championship game.

6 Steve Young's 6 TD passes in a Super Bowl

Throwing six touchdown passes in a game has been done 47 times since 1950. Throwing six in the Super Bowl? Steve Young is the only QB to pull that off. Young threw 51-, 44-, 15-, eight-, seven-, and five-yard scoring strikes in the San Francisco 49ers' 49–26 victory over the San Diego Chargers in Super Bowl XXIX.

7 Brett Favre's 321 consecutive starts

Between the start of Brett Favre's streak in 1992 and its end in 2010, the NFL added four teams and four men served as President of the United States. The quarterback didn't just show up, he performed, leading his teams to the playoffs 12 times in 19 seasons and winning Super Bowl XXXI.

8 Derrick Thomas's 7 sacks in a game

On November 12, 1990, the Kansas City Chiefs' Derrick Thomas spent all day harassing Seattle Seahawks QB Dave Krieg. Unfortunately, Thomas missed an eighth sack, which proved costly. Krieg shook Thomas loose to throw the game-winning touchdown pass as time expired.

9 Calvin Johnson's 1,964 receiving yards in a season

In 2012, Johnson became the first player in NFL history to rack up more than 1,900 receiving yards in a season, breaking legend Jerry Rice's previous record of 1,848 (a mark that had stood for 17 years). With teams spreading the ball around to different receivers, no one else has made it to even 1,700 yards since 2002.

10 Eric Dickerson's 2,105 rushing yards in a season

The Los Angeles Rams running back piled up 12 100-yard games and two 200-yard games in 1984. The NFL's trend of splitting carries among multiple backs means that a player likely won't get the workload Eric Dickerson enjoyed in '84.

Top 10 Big Guys

1

Ed (Too Tall) Jones
Defensive End
HT: 6'9" WT: 271 lbs

On the field and in the ring, Ed (Too Tall) Jones used his size to his advantage. One of the tallest players ever to play in the NFL, he was a key member of the Dallas Cowboys' Doomsday Defense and played in three Super Bowls. After five years with the Cowboys, he tried his hand at boxing. Jones sat out the 1979 NFL season and won all of his bouts before returning to the Cowboys the following year. He went on to become a Pro Bowler from 1981 through '83 and ranked among the top 10 in the league in sacks in 1985 and '87.

2 Orlando Pace *Left Tackle*
HT: 6'7" WT: 325 lbs

While playing for the St. Louis Rams, Orlando Pace was a giant and fierce blocker for NFL MVPs Kurt Warner and Marshall Faulk. He started 154 games as a key member of the Rams' offensive line. From 1999 through 2008, St. Louis was second in the NFL in points (24.2 per game) and total offense (361 yards per game).

3 Jerome Bettis *Running Back*
HT: 5'11" WT: 255 lbs

Jerome Bettis was built like his nickname, Bus. The hefty runner often carried — and ran over — multiple defenders on the field. A six-time Pro Bowler and Hall of Famer, Bettis was the NFL's fifth-leading rusher of all time when he retired (13,662 yards over 13 seasons in the league).

4 Jonathan Ogden *Left Tackle*
HT: 6'9" WT: 345 lbs

Jonathan Ogden's colossal size helped him dominate defensive ends, and his swift feet and athleticism made him a staple of the Baltimore Ravens' offensive line. A leader of the 2000 Super Bowl champs, Ogden made 11 Pro Bowl appearances during his 12-year career.

5 **Kris Jenkins** *Nose Tackle*
HT: 6'4" WT: 360 lbs
A sturdy run-stuffer and pass-rushing threat, Kris Jenkins used his massive build to disrupt backfields. Jenkins played in four Pro Bowls and anchored the defenses of the Carolina Panthers (2001–07) and the New York Jets (2008–10) before knee injuries slowed down his career.

6 **Casey Hampton** *Nose Tackle*
HT: 6'1" WT: 325 lbs
Nicknamed Big Snack, Casey Hampton has devoured opponents. In 12 seasons with the Pittsburgh Steelers, Hampton helped the team lead the league in run defense four times (and finish in the top three in run D 10 times). His ability to clog the middle earned him trips to five Pro Bowls.

7 **Gilbert Brown** *Nose Tackle*
HT: 6'2" WT: 340 lbs
Thanks in large part to Gilbert Brown, the Green Bay Packers allowed the fewest touchdowns in the NFL in 1996 (19) and went on to win the Super Bowl. Brown, who wore a size-66 jacket, was also the inspiration for a sandwich at a local Burger King: The Gilbertburger was a Double Whopper with a double helping of toppings.

8 **Vince Wilfork** *Nose Tackle*
HT: 6'2" WT: 325 lbs
While Tom Brady led the offense for the great Patriots teams of the 2000s, it was the massive Wilfork who anchored the defense. He helped New England to two Super Bowl championships and two other title game appearances, while making the Pro Bowl five times.

9 **Aaron Gibson** *Right Tackle*
HT: 6'6" WT: 375 lbs
Aaron Gibson is the heaviest player in NFL history (he weighed as much as 440 pounds during his playing career). During his eight seasons in the league, he played for the Detroit Lions, Dallas Cowboys, and Chicago Bears. Gibson wore an 8⅜-sized helmet, thought to be the largest ever manufactured by Riddell.

10 **Leonard Davis** *Guard/Tackle*
HT: 6'6" WT: 375 lbs
The Arizona Cardinals made Davis the second overall pick of the 2001 draft, but it wasn't until he signed with the Dallas Cowboys in 2007 that he truly hit it big. A mauling run-blocker, he made the Pro Bowl in each of his first three seasons in Dallas.

Top 10 **Little Guys**

1 **Barry Sanders**
Running Back
HT: 5'8" WT: 200 lbs
Quick and agile, Barry Sanders is among the greatest running backs in NFL history. He led the NFL in rushing four times, including his 2,053-yard effort in 1997 for the Detroit Lions. Sanders retired after 10 seasons, when he was second on the all-time rushing list (15,269 yards).

2 **Drew Brees**
Quarterback
HT: 6'0" WT: 209 lbs
Drew Brees was considered too small for the NFL and slipped to the second round of the 2001 draft. But he emerged as a quality starter for the San Diego Chargers and then became a superstar for the New Orleans Saints. He was named MVP of Super Bowl XLIV after leading the Saints to their first championship.

3 **Darrell Green**
Cornerback
HT: 5'9" WT: 185 lbs
Almost every receiver Darrell Green faced was taller than he was, but his blazing speed and football smarts made him one of the greatest shutdown corners of all time. Starring for the Washington Redskins in the 1980s and '90s, Green won two Super Bowls, made seven Pro Bowls, and played his way into the Hall of Fame.

4 **Sam Mills**
Linebacker
HT: 5'9" WT: 232 lbs
In part due to his height, Sam Mills didn't even make an NFL team early in his career and was cut from a CFL roster. He later starred in the USFL and got the attention of the New Orleans Saints. Nicknamed Field Mouse, Mills became the heart of the Saints' defense in the 1980s and '90s and made the Pro Bowl five times.

5 **Steve Smith Sr.**
Wide Receiver
HT: 5'9" WT: 185 lbs
While most small receivers specialize in catching short passes, Steve Smith's speed and toughness made him one of the NFL's most dangerous deep threats. In 2005, he tied for first in receptions (103) and TD catches (12) and led the NFL in receiving yards (1,563). He made the Pro Bowl five times.

6 Maurice Jones-Drew
Running Back
HT: 5'7" WT: 208 lbs

Maurice Jones-Drew is short, but he has a thick, muscular build and enormous leg strength, allowing him to get low and push through piles. The Jacksonville Jaguars' three-time Pro Bowler won the NFL rushing crown in 2011 (1,606 yards) and scored 10 or more touchdowns in a season four times in his career.

7 Bob Sanders
Safety
HT: 5'8" WT: 206 lbs

Bob Sanders packed a lot of power into his tiny frame and became one of the most feared hitters in his prime. The 2007 NFL Defensive Player of the Year, Sanders roamed the middle of the field for the Indianapolis Colts and used his great instincts to put himself in the right place at exactly the right time.

8 Wes Welker
Wide Receiver
HT: 5'9" WT: 185 lbs

Wes Welker was a relatively unknown player when the New England Patriots acquired him in 2007, but the shifty slot receiver quickly became QB Tom Brady's favorite target. A five-time Pro Bowler, Welker tied for the NFL lead in receptions in 2007 (112) and led the league in '09 (123) and '11 (122).

9 Buddy Young
Running Back
HT: 5'4" WT: 175 lbs

Buddy Young was a multi-purpose threat for the New York Yanks, Dallas Texans, and Baltimore Colts during the early days of the NFL. A running back, receiver, and return man, he was often impossible for defenders to catch. He led the NFL in yards per touch (10.7) in 1949 and made the Pro Bowl in 1954.

10 Doug Flutie
Quarterback
HT: 5'10" WT: 180 lbs

Doug Flutie spent most of his career in the Canadian Football League before finally taking off in the NFL with the Buffalo Bills in 1998. Even though he had trouble seeing over his offensive line, Flutie relied on his scrambling ability to lead the Bills to the playoffs in '98 and '99.

TOP 10
WACKY
WEAT
GAMES

Y
HER

1

Philadelphia Eagles at Chicago Bears
December 31, 1988

The Bears had just gone up 17–6 against the Eagles in their Wild Card playoff matchup when, suddenly, everything went black . . . er, white. In the second quarter, a fog rolled in, filling Chicago's Soldier Field. In the game forever known as the Fog Bowl, visibility on the field was limited to 10 to 15 yards, which made it nearly impossible for either team to advance the ball very far. Fans — both at the game and watching on TV — couldn't see a thing. Referee Jim Tunney used his microphone to announce the down and distance before every play, trying to help viewers follow along. Chicago held on for a 20–12 win, leading one Bears fan to remark: "Best game I've never seen!"

2 Dallas Cowboys at Green Bay Packers
December 31, 1967

▼ Known as the Ice Bowl, the 1967 NFL Championship was the coldest game on record (game-time temperature was –13°). But it was also one of the greatest games ever played, capped off by Packers quarterback Bart Starr's lunging forward for a touchdown in the final seconds to secure a 21–17 win.

3 Tampa Bay Buccaneers at Green Bay Packers
December 1, 1985

It takes a lot to keep Packers fans away from Lambeau Field, but the team's stadium was two thirds empty for this 1985 game because a foot of snow had fallen in Wisconsin. Another six inches came down during the game. Even though the Bucs' white uniforms blended in with the snowy background, it was no surprise when the team from Florida fell short, losing 21–0.

6 Chicago Cardinals at Philadelphia Eagles
December 19, 1948

▼ At kickoff of the 1948 NFL Championship game, snow was falling at a rate of two inches per hour. The grounds crew had to ask the players from both teams to help remove it. The game's only score came when Philly halfback Steve Van Buren ran the ball into the end zone with 1:05 left, giving the Eagles a 7–0 win.

7 San Diego Chargers at Cincinnati Bengals
January 10, 1982

► The Ice Bowl (*see Number 2*) might have been the lowest temperature ever recorded for an NFL game, but if you factor in wind chill, nothing tops the Freezer Bowl. The temperature was –9° for the 1982 AFC championship, but with the wind whipping through Riverfront Stadium it felt like –59 degrees. Coming from sunny California, quarterback Dan Fouts and the Chargers weren't ready for that kind of cold. The Bengals rolled easily, winning 27–7.

4 Kansas City Chiefs at Tampa Bay Buccaneers

December 16, 1979

► In 1979, the only thing wackier than the thought of the lowly Bucs making the playoffs for the first time in franchise history was the weather during their clinching game. The rain fell so hard that it looked like waterfalls. In a sloppy game, the Bucs scored a late field goal for a 3–0 victory and their first trip to the playoffs.

9 Green Bay Packers at Arizona Cardinals

September 21, 2003

◄ The Packers have played in a lot of cold-weather classics, but they got the other end of the spectrum when they visited Sun Devil Stadium in 2003. The temperature on the field was 102 degrees at kickoff and eventually reached 106. The heat helped the Cardinals cool off the Packers in a 20–13 upset win.

8 Miami Dolphins at New England Patriots

December 12, 1982

► A snowstorm on game day piled snow atop an already icy surface. Late in the fourth quarter of a scoreless game, the snow plow controversy took place: With the Pats setting up for a field goal, a grounds crew worker went to clear the yard line, but then veered to clean the area where the ball would be held. Miami coach Don Shula protested but was told nothing could be done. The cleared spot helped Pats kicker John Smith split the uprights for the game's only points.

5 New York Giants at St. Louis Cardinals

November 15, 1964

▼ NFL Films called it the muddiest game in NFL history. Rain and a sloppy field made the Cards' white uniforms and the Giants' blue ones brown by the end of a fumble-filled 10–10 tie.

10 Oakland Raiders at New England Patriots

January 19, 2002

▲ With four inches of snow covering the field at Foxboro Stadium, the Pats got a miracle when a Tom Brady fumble that would have ended the game was overturned on review. Five plays later, Adam Vinatieri nailed a 45-yard field goal to force overtime, and then added a short field goal in OT for a 16–13 Pats win.

2 **White football**
Until the mid-1950s, the NFL would occasionally use a white ball for night games. At the time, stadium lighting wasn't that bright, so a normal ball was hard to see in the dark. The white ball, which debuted in 1931, stood out for players and fans. The balls were completely white until 1941, when black stripes were added at the ends.

1 **Football warmer**
Legendary coach Paul Brown of the Cleveland Browns tried this electric ball warmer in the 1950s, according to Jason Aikens, the collections curator at the Pro Football Hall of Fame. Brown wanted a warm ball that would be easier to handle in cold games. Unfortunately, the device worked a little too well. One of the first footballs Brown put in the warmer got cooked. The ball was unusable, and probably wouldn't have tasted good, either. The experiment was soon abandoned.

5 **Oldest football in the Pro Football Hall of Fame**
Footballs from the early days of the game, such as this one from around 1895, were rounder and shaped like melons. In the late 1800s, players did not throw or carry the ball. Instead, they kicked it to score points. It wasn't until 1906 that the forward pass was introduced.

Top 10 Artifacts

3 Tom Dempsey's shoe
Born without toes on his right foot, New Orleans Saints kicker Tom Dempsey wore a custom-made shoe when he came out for field goals. Dempsey booted a 63-yard field goal in 1970, the longest in NFL history. (Jason Elam of the Denver Broncos tied the record in 1998.)

4 Football ticket
In 2010, the average NFL ticket price was $76.47. The New England Patriots had the highest average ($118) and the Cleveland Browns had the lowest ($55). It's certainly a far cry from the 1937 season, when $2.20 would buy you a lower-tier seat to a football game between the Brooklyn Dodgers and Philadelphia Eagles. (The Dodgers were at the losing end of this game, 14–10.)

6 Joe Namath's knee brace
New York Jets quarterback Joe Namath had struggled with bad knees since college and underwent four knee operations while in the NFL. Thanks to knee braces, including this one that he wore in 1967, Namath was able to prolong his pro career, which lasted 13 seasons.

7 Football jacket
In 1895, players really felt it when they were hit. The only shock absorbers they had were a heavy canvas vest and a jacket.

8 Leather helmet
The NFL didn't require players to wear head gear until 1943, but even then there wasn't a lot of protection. Early helmets, like this one belonging to the 1949 Chicago Cardinals, were made of leather. The facemask wasn't invented until the 1930s.

9 Shoulder pads
Modern shoulder pads feature a plastic shell over thick foam padding that can withstand the brutal collisions of today's game. But around 1920, shoulder pads like these were made of little more than cotton felt and leather.

10 Ring from Super Bowl I
Featuring just a single diamond, the ring that members of the Green Bay Packers took home for winning the first Super Bowl has less bling than today's models. Coach Vince Lombardi had a hand in designing the ring, which included some unique details. In addition to the scores of the conference championship game and the Super Bowl, it has a crown with the Lombardi family crest that states HARMONY, COURAGE, VALOR.

Top 10 Lovable Losers

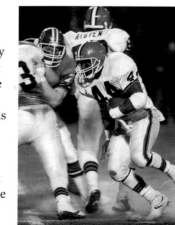

Detroit Lions

Some Detroit fans think the *l* in Lions might stand for *losing*. In 2008, Detroit made history as the first team to go 0–16. Even though the Lions have been in the NFL for the entire Super Bowl era, they've never played in the big game. They've played in only one conference championship (in 1992) . . . and lost by 31 points. The Lions were so luckless that they couldn't even hang on to their biggest star, Hall of Fame running back Barry Sanders, who retired in 1999 at the age of 31 after a 1,491-yard season.

2 Cleveland Browns

► The Browns have never played in a Super Bowl despite coming agonizingly close in the late 1980s. They lost in the AFC Championship Game to the Denver Broncos in 1986, '87, and '89. The 1987 season was perhaps the most painful: The Browns were driving to tie the score late in the game, but then Cleveland running back Earnest Byner fumbled the ball inside the Denver five-yard line with less than 30 seconds to play.

3 Minnesota Vikings

Playoff woes have plagued Minnesota for decades. Quarterback Fran Tarkenton led a quality Vikings offense to four Super Bowls from 1970 to '77 — but the team collapsed every time, averaging less than nine points a game in four Super Bowl losses. In 1998 the Vikings went 15–1 but didn't make the Super Bowl because their kicker missed his first field goal of the season with two minutes to go in the NFC Championship Game.

4 Buffalo Bills

The Bills are the only team to play in four consecutive Super Bowls (1991–94). Unfortunately, they lost them all. The franchise has never won a Super Bowl title in its 51-year existence. Through 2010 the Bills are tied for the league's longest active playoff drought, with no trips to the playoffs since the 1999 season.

5 Cincinnati Bengals

The Bengals have made only nine playoff appearances in their 42-year franchise history. Cincy missed the playoffs every season from 1991 through 2004, a stretch in which the team was 82 games under .500. Even when the Bengals are good, fans know it won't last. They've made the playoffs in back-to-back seasons only once.

6 Tampa Bay Buccaneers

▲ When you see classic bloopers from the NFL, the majority of the lowlights involve players in ugly, Creamsicle-orange uniforms. Those were the Bucs. The franchise debuted in 1976 and immediately staked a claim as the worst team in the league. In its first two seasons, Tampa Bay won two games total.

7 Houston Oilers/ Tennessee Titans

In their first two years of existence (1960 and '61), the Houston Oilers won back-to-back AFL league championships. The franchise — which moved to Tennessee in 1997 and became the Titans two years later — hasn't won a title since. In 1993, the Oilers suffered one of the most famous playoff defeats in history: They blew a 35–3 second-half lead over the Bills in the Wild Card round and lost 41–38.

8 Arizona Cardinals

◄ The Cardinals have been around since 1920 but have never won a Super Bowl. Since 1976, the franchise has finished the regular season with double-digit wins only once.

9 New Orleans Saints

A Super Bowl XLIV win can't erase the painful early years of the Saints. It took New Orleans 21 seasons to make its first playoff appearance, and 14 more to get its first playoff win. In 1980, the Saints went 1–15, prompting fans to nickname the team the Aints.

10 San Diego Chargers

The Chargers have won a lot of regular-season games, but come playoff time, they're a different team. In 2004 the Chargers had the best record in the NFL, only to lose at home in the first round of the playoffs. In 2009 the Chargers closed out the season with 11 straight wins, only to lose at home again in the first round. The Bolts have never won a Super Bowl, losing by 23 in their lone big-game appearance, in 1995.

Kurt Warner
Quarterback (1998–2009)

Kurt Warner was the ultimate underdog. In college, he didn't start for Northern Iowa until his senior year, and then he went undrafted. The Green Bay Packers invited him to training camp only to cut him, so Warner worked at a grocery store stocking shelves. He went on to play for the Arena Football League's Iowa Barnstormers from 1995 through '97. Then in 1998 he got another shot at the NFL when he signed with the St. Louis Rams, backing up starter Trent Green. When Green was injured during the 1999 preseason, Warner stepped in — and became an all-time great. In his first season as a starter, he was league MVP and Super Bowl MVP. Warner played 12 NFL seasons, in which he won two MVP awards, made four Pro Bowls, and led two teams (the Rams and the Arizona Cardinals) to the Super Bowl.

Top 10 Undrafted Players

2 Warren Moon
Quarterback (1984–2000)
Scouts wanted Warren Moon to move to tight end; he refused and was undrafted in 1978. Moon starred in the Canadian Football League before signing with the Houston Oilers in 1984 and leading a dangerous passing attack. The Hall of Famer ranks fifth all-time in career passing yards (49,325).

3 James Harrison
Linebacker (2002–present)
Teams thought that James Harrison was too small (6' 0", 242 pounds) to play in the NFL. He was cut four times before catching on as a Steelers' special-teamer. From there, he became the first undrafted player to win NFL Defensive Player of the Year, in 2008.

4 John Randle
Defensive Tackle (1990–2003)
An undersized tackle coming out of Texas A&M–Kingsville, John Randle got little attention leading up to the 1990 NFL Draft. He signed with the Vikings as a reserve and later became one of the most disruptive linemen of all time. Randle was elected to the Hall of Fame in 2010.

5 Larry Little
Guard (1967–80)
Undrafted out of tiny Bethune-Cookman, Larry Little signed with the Chargers in 1967 but was traded to Miami in 1969. With the Dolphins, he developed into a Hall of Fame blocker. He paved the way for Miami's mighty ground game, helping the Dolphins win two Super Bowls.

6 Antonio Gates
Tight End (2003–present)
Even though he was a high school football star, Antonio Gates didn't play the sport in college. Instead, he played basketball at Kent State. Not built for the NBA, the 6' 4" Gates returned to football. The Chargers signed him as a free agent in 2003, and he's rewarded them with eight Pro Bowl seasons.

7 Jason Peters
Offensive Tackle (2004–present)
A tight end at Arkansas, Jason Peters wasn't much of a pass catcher. The Bills signed him in 2004, and a year later he was a full-time offensive lineman. By '06, Peters was starting at left tackle and has become one of the NFL's elite blockers, first for Buffalo and then for the Eagles.

8 Tony Romo
Quarterback (2003–present)
Undrafted out of Eastern Illinois, the Cowboys signed Tony Romo and kept him on the bench for more than three seasons. Since stepping in as the starter in Dallas, he has become a bona fide star. He has made four Pro Bowls and led the Cowboys to the playoffs four times.

9 Brian Waters
Guard (2000–13)
A tight end at North Texas, Brian Waters was forced to switch positions in the NFL. The Cowboys cut him in 1999, but the Chiefs gave him a chance in 2000 after he played well in NFL Europe. Waters became a starter in 2001 and has since made six Pro Bowls and two All-Pro teams.

10 Priest Holmes
Running Back (1997–2007)
Priest Holmes caught on with the Ravens as a special-teamer in 1997 and later earned a roll as a third-down back. But it wasn't until he joined the Chiefs in 2001 that he became a household name, making three All-Pro teams and winning Offensive Player of the Year in 2002.

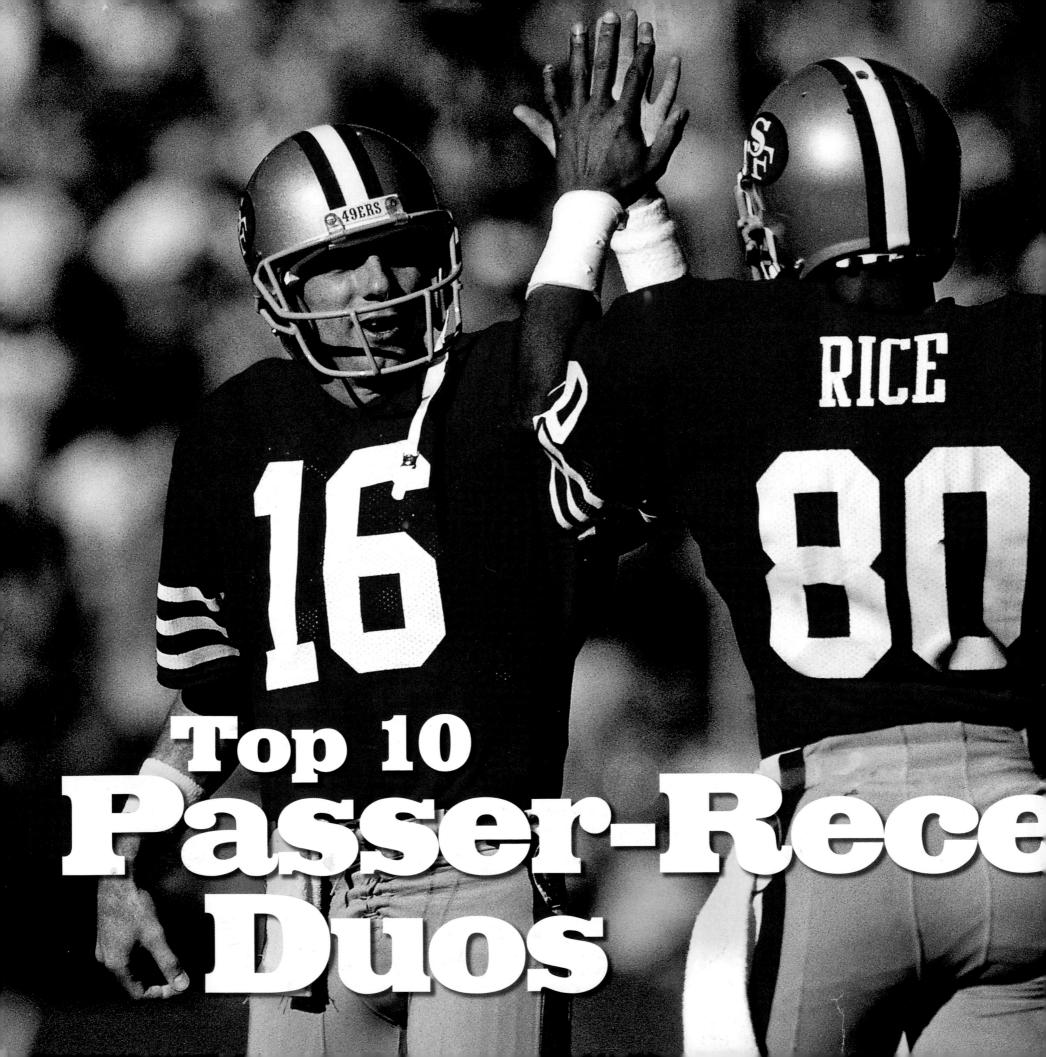

Top 10
Passer-Rece
Duos

1
Joe Montana and Jerry Rice,
San Francisco 49ers

They won two Super Bowls together and each took home an MVP award in the big game — Jerry Rice in Super Bowl XXIII, Joe Montana in Super Bowl XXIV. From 1985 through '90, the teammates connected for more than 7,000 yards. They are the best ever at their respective positions, so it's no surprise that both have busts in the Pro Football Hall of Fame.

iver

2
Steve Young and Jerry Rice,
San Francisco 49ers

In 1992, Steve Young was in the tough position of taking over at quarterback for 49ers legend Joe Montana. But Young immediately formed a connection with Jerry Rice. From 1992 through '98 San Francisco had the most passing yards and points in the league and didn't miss the postseason over that span. The Niners won it all in 1994, with Young earning Super Bowl MVP honors.

YOUNG RICE

3
Terry Bradshaw and Lynn Swann,
Pittsburgh Steelers

It was all about big plays in the big game between these two Steelers Hall of Famers. In three Super Bowls, Terry Bradshaw and Lynn Swann connected for more than 360 yards, with three touchdowns. Thanks to Bradshaw's strong arm and Swann's ability to catch the deep ball, the two averaged 43 yards per Super Bowl touchdown.

BRADSHAW SWANN

4
Johnny Unitas and Raymond Berry,
Baltimore Colts

These two basically invented the two-minute offense and timing routes. Johnny Unitas threw a total of 63 touchdown passes to Raymond Berry. The teammates were known for their preparation on the practice field and were nearly unstoppable on game days. In the 1958 NFL Championship, Unitas found Berry 12 times for 178 yards and a touchdown to lead the Colts to their first league title.

UNITAS BERRY

5
Troy Aikman and Michael Irvin,
Dallas Cowboys

Troy Aikman was a steady leader, and Michael Irvin was a flashy showman. Together they wound up with numerous Super Bowl rings and their names in the Hall of Fame. The two combined for 49 touchdowns and led Dallas to three Super Bowl victories from 1992 through '95.

AIKMAN IRVIN

6
Ken Stabler and Fred Biletnikoff,
Oakland Raiders

When Ken Stabler needed a big play, he knew he could count on Fred Biletnikoff. The Raiders rode the duo all the way to win Super Bowl XI. Biletnikoff was named the game's MVP for making key catches on three scoring drives.

STABLER BILETNIKOFF

7
Peyton Manning and Marvin Harrison, *Indianapolis Colts*

Peyton Manning's first NFL TD pass was to Marvin Harrison. The two would hook up for 111 more touchdowns from 1998 through 2008, more than any other QB-wideout combo in NFL history.

MANNING HARRISON

8
Tom Brady and Randy Moss,
New England Patriots

In 2007, Tom Brady and Randy Moss had the most prolific passing and receiving season in NFL history. Brady set a record by tossing 50 touchdown passes. Moss caught a record 23 scoring passes.

BRADY MOSS

9
Dan Marino and Mark Clayton,
Miami Dolphins

Dan Marino and Mark Clayton entered the league together with the Dolphins in 1983. By the time Clayton left the team after the '92 season, the two had combined for 79 TDs. Clayton caught more than 500 passes for over 8,000 yards from Marino.

MARINO CLAYTON

10
Daunte Culpepper and Randy Moss, *Minnesota Vikings*

From 2000 through '04, it was hard to find a more dangerous deep-play threat. Of the 53 touchdown passes Daunte Culpepper threw to Randy Moss, 21 covered 30 yards or more.

CULPEPPER MOSS

Top 10 Coaches

1 Vince Lombardi
Green Bay Packers (1959–67),
Washington Redskins (1969)

After being hired as the Packers' head coach in 1959, Vince Lombardi delivered a powerful message to the team, which had finished with an embarrassing 1–10–1 record the previous season. "I have never been on a losing team, gentlemen, and I do not intend to start now," he said. Two seasons later the Packers won the first of five championship titles during his nine seasons at the helm. Lombardi was a leader and a technician, equally skilled at delivering a motivational speech and crafting an offensive play. He went 89–29–4 in Green Bay before departing for Washington in 1969, where he led the Redskins to their first winning season in 14 years.

2 Don Shula *Baltimore Colts (1963–69), Miami Dolphins (1970–95)*

The winningest coach in NFL history, Don Shula finished with a record below .500 only twice in 33 seasons. After seven consecutive winning seasons with the Colts, he won two Super Bowls with the Dolphins and led them to a historic 17–0 season in 1972.

3 Paul Brown *Cleveland Browns (1946–62), Cincinnati Bengals (1968–75)*

Paul Brown created a dynasty in Cleveland — four All-America Football Conference championships, three NFL titles, and a 158–48–8 record. In 17 years, Cleveland had only one losing season under Brown, who has been called the father of the modern offense.

4 Chuck Noll *Pittsburgh Steelers (1969–91)*

His 1969 team was a dismal 1–13, but three seasons later Chuck Noll turned the Steelers around, leading them to an 11–3 record and the AFC Central Division title. Noll is the only coach to win four Super Bowls without a loss in the big game, and he was the mastermind behind Pittsburgh's famous Steel Curtain defense.

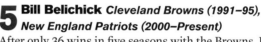

5 Bill Belichick *Cleveland Browns (1991–95), New England Patriots (2000–Present)*

After only 36 wins in five seasons with the Browns, Bill Belichick began his career in New England with a 5–11 record in 2000. That would be his last losing season. A defensive wizard, he went on to lead the Patriots to four Super Bowl titles.

6 Joe Gibbs *Washington Redskins (1981–92, 2004–07)*

Joe Gibbs is the only coach in NFL history to win three championships with three different quarterbacks. Under Gibbs, the Redskins dominated the line of scrimmage with a tough offensive line. A three-time NFL Coach of the Year, he is one of only eight coaches to lead his team to four Super Bowl appearances.

7 George Halas *Chicago Bears (1920–29, 1933–42, 1946–55, 1958–67)*

Known as Papa Bear, George Halas was the face of the Bears for decades. He led Chicago to six titles in his 40-year career and was the first coach to hold daily practice and use game film to study opponents. Halas's 318 wins rank second all-time behind Don Shula.

8 Tom Landry *Dallas Cowboys (1960–88)*

Wearing his trademark fedora, Tom Landry was a technical innovator who introduced the flex defense (a variation of a 4–3) and the multiple offense (a strategy that uses several formations). A two-time Super Bowl champion, Landry led Dallas to 20 consecutive winning seasons and five NFC championships.

9 Bill Parcells *New York Giants (1983–90), New England Patriots (1993–96), New York Jets (1997–99), Dallas Cowboys (2003–06)*

Wherever he went, Bill Parcells found a way to win. He is the only coach to take four different franchises to the playoffs. Known for his no-nonsense attitude, Parcells won two Super Bowls with the Giants.

10 Curly Lambeau *Green Bay Packers (1921–49), Chicago Cardinals (1950–51), Washington Redskins (1952–53)*

Curly Lambeau established the Packers in 1919, before the NFL even existed. He served as both coach and general manager of the team and became the first coach to make the forward pass an offensive staple. Lambeau's teams won six championships.

1 Instant reply

► The NFL started using instant replay to review calls in 1986. Back then, only the on-field officials could ask for a replay, which would then be reviewed by an official in the booth. The system was lengthy and often inconclusive, so the NFL scrapped it before the 1992 season. But the league brought back an improved instant replay in 1999. Now, coaches are allowed two challenges per game — and a third if their first two challenges prove correct — and a booth official is in charge of calling for reviews in the final two minutes of each half. With all the different angles available, referees, who use a sideline monitor to view replays, should (in theory) get the call right.

Top 10 Technical Innovations

2 Face masks

◄ Vern McMillan, a sporting-goods store owner from Terre Haute, Indiana, is most often credited with inventing the football face mask in the mid-1930s. Legendary quarterback Otto Graham was one of the first players to wear it. In 1953, coach Paul Brown attached a protective strip of plastic to Graham's helmet after his QB's face was bloodied by an elbow.

3 Arthroscopic surgery

Dr. Robert Jackson brought arthroscopy to sports in the 1970s. The surgery involves inserting a tiny camera to view damage to a joint, which allows doctors to diagnose injuries more accurately. If no major damage is found, players can return to action quickly.

4 Video screens

► The Louisiana Superdome had the NFL's first giant video screen, in 1975. But that one looks tiny compared with the 600-ton Jumbotron in the Cowboys' AT&T Stadium.

5 Helmet radios

► In 1956, the Cleveland Browns became the first team to use a helmet radio, allowing coaches to send in plays from the sideline without hand signals. However, the NFL outlawed it soon after. In 1994, the league decided that teams could use one-way communication devices in the quarterback's helmet, and in 2008, defenses were allowed to choose one player to receive defensive calls.

6 Yellow line for first down

▼ It used to be awfully tough for fans watching on TV to tell if their team had just made a first down. But in 1998, the 1st & Ten graphics system put that magic yellow line on the field for TV viewers.

7 FieldTurf

First installed at Seattle's Qwest (now CenturyLink) Field, FieldTurf quickly became the NFL's artificial surface of choice. AstroTurf was often blamed for injuries and criticized for its lack of cushioning. FieldTurf is much more like natural grass, allowing players to cut with confidence and get right back up after a hard landing.

8 RedZone channel

If you've ever been lucky enough to watch DirecTV's NFL package on Sundays, you probably spent a lot of time on the RedZone channel. It switches among games all day, showing you the matchup in which a team is closest to scoring.

9 Playbooks on Tablets

► The pages of playbooks aren't made of paper anymore. Now, tablet devices such as the Microsoft Surface allow players and coaches to study past plays and draw up new ones right on the sideline.

10 Domed stadiums

Houston's Astrodome was the NFL's first domed stadium, allowing massive amounts of fans to watch football in the comfort of an indoor arena. In 2015, eight NFL teams play in domed stadiums, four of which had retractable roofs.

Top 10 Football Families

1 Peyton, Archie, and Eli Manning

The Mannings are the First Family of quarterbacks. Dad Archie was a legend at the University of Mississippi, before the New Orleans Saints chose him second overall in the 1971 draft. He made two Pro Bowls despite playing for some of the worst teams in history. Archie's middle son, Peyton, brought the family QB legacy to new heights: In 18 seasons, he has been named to 14 Pro Bowls and was the MVP of Super Bowl XLI with the Indianapolis Colts. For a while, Eli was known only as the little brother, but he broke out in Super Bowl XLII, leading one of the greatest drives in the championship's history to upset the then-undefeated New England Patriots. He won a second title in Super Bowl XLVI, and Peyton got his second ring in Super Bowl 50.

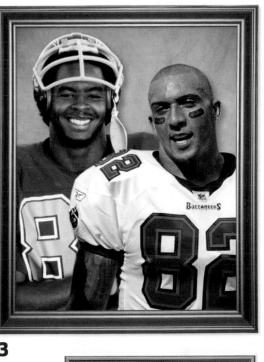

2 Bruce, Clay Jr., and Clay III Matthews
Bruce is a Hall of Fame offensive lineman. His older brother, Clay Jr., is a four-time Pro Bowl linebacker. And Clay Jr.'s son Clay III is a five-time Pro Bowl linebacker for the Packers who won the family's first Super Bowl, in 2011.

3 Kellen and Kellen II Winslow
During the 1980s, Hall of Famer Kellen Winslow was a tight end with a reputation for great hands and toughness. The same was said about his son Kellen Winslow II 25 years later. Together, they combined for 1,010 catches and six Pro Bowls.

4 Sterling and Shannon Sharpe
Sterling, a wide receiver for the Packers, had 8,134 receiving yards and made five Pro Bowls from 1988 through '94. Little brother Shannon is one of four tight ends with more than 10,000 receiving yards and was inducted into the Hall of Fame in 2011.

5 Ronde and Tiki Barber
These twins caused trouble, one on each side of the ball. In 16 seasons, Ronde, a cornerback, made 47 interceptions and five Pro Bowls. Tiki, a running back, had six 1,000-yard rushing seasons and led the NFL in yards from scrimmage in 2004 and '05.

6 Jim and John Harbaugh
These brothers coached against each other in Super Bowl XLVII; John's Ravens topped Jim's 49ers, 34–31. Jim left to coach the University of Michigan after the 2014 season. At the time, both brothers had won more than 60% of their games as NFL coaches.

7 Randall and Sam Cunningham
Sam was a bruising runner, pounding out 5,453 rushing yards for the Patriots from 1973 through '82. Brother Randall, 13 years younger, was a dynamic QB. He could beat teams with his arm (29,979 career passing yards) *and* his legs (4,928 rushing yards).

8 Dale Carter and Jake Reed
These brothers (Jake changed his last name after their parents divorced) were on opposite sides of the passing game. Jake, a wideout, had four 1,000-yard receiving seasons for the Vikings in the 1990s. Dale was a star cornerback for the Chiefs during that time.

9 Howie, Chris and Jake Long
Howie Long was a Hall of Fame defensive end for the Raiders in the 1980s. His son Chris became a star pass rusher for the Rams. Chris's brother Kyle, on the other hand, plays on the offensive line, where he made the Pro Bowl in each of his first two seasons.

10 Vernon and Vontae Davis
Vernon, a tight end, was a first-round pick of the 49ers in 2006, and three years later Miami took his brother Vontae, a cornerback, in Round 1. Both lived up to their billing. Vernon made two Pro Bowls, while Vontae has made one since a trade to the Colts.

Top 10
Touchdown

Celebrations

Lambeau Leap

This Green Bay Packers celebration got its start in 1993, when safety LeRoy Butler returned a fumble for a touchdown at Lambeau Field. After running through the end zone, Butler leaped up against the stadium's padded wall. He made it only halfway up the wall when fans reached over and held Butler up for a couple of joyous seconds. The Lambeau Leap has been a tradition ever since.

2 The Ickey Shuffle

During the Cincinnati Bengals' surprising Super Bowl run in 1988, one of the biggest stars on the team was rookie running back Ickey Woods. He tied for the AFC lead in touchdowns that year, but he was known more for what he did after he scored: the Ickey Shuffle. A stutter step to the right, a stutter step to the left, repeat it twice, and then a big spike. To finish the Shuffle, Woods added a finger twirl and some hip-shaking.

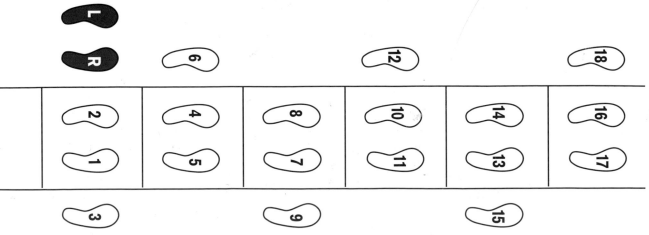

3 The Fun Bunch

In the early 1980s, this group of Washington Redskins made celebrating a team effort with its group high fives after touchdowns. The Fun Bunch was created by the Redskins' receiving corps, including Hall of Famer Art Monk, but its routines caused the NFL to create a rule banning excessive celebrations in 1984.

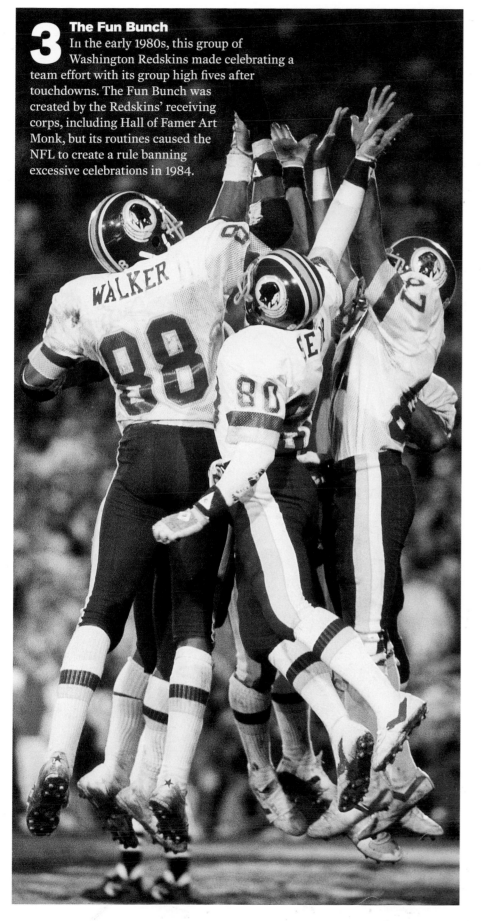

4 The Mile High Salute

Denver Broncos running back Terrell Davis popularized this celebration during the team's Super Bowl–winning seasons (1997 and '98). He created the move as a tribute to his father, who served in the military. Davis led the NFL in rushing TDs during that span, so he had plenty of chances to salute.

5 The Finger Roll

This celebration should look familiar, considering LaDainian Tomlinson scored the third-most touchdowns in NFL history, and set the single-season TD record in 2006 (31). Once LT got into the end zone, he would put one hand behind his head while letting the ball coolly roll off the fingers of his other hand.

6 The Dirty Bird

The 1998 Atlanta Falcons advanced to the Super Bowl, led by running back Jamal Anderson. Anderson finished the season with 1,846 rushing yards, 16 total TDs, and one memorable dance. Whenever Anderson scored, he would bounce lightly from foot to foot while bending his arms at the elbows and flapping them like a bird. The celebration became known as the Dirty Bird, and it wasn't long before Anderson's teammates got in on the act.

7 The Best of Ochocinco

Chad Johnson (aka Chad Ochocinco) has too many elaborate TD celebrations to pick just one. You like dancing? He performed everything from traditional Irish step dancing to the Chicken Dance. You want props? Johnson showed off multiple homemade signs and once took control of a network TV camera. You want fan involvement? Johnson jumped into both home and away crowds and even faked a marriage proposal to a cheerleader. His celebrations were so exciting that they almost overshadowed the touchdowns that preceded them.

9 **Slam Dunk**
Tony Gonzalez will likely be inducted into the Pro Football Hall of Fame one day, but he also excelled at basketball in college. (His Cal team advanced to the Sweet 16 of the NCAA tournament in 1997.) As a nod to his hoops days, Gonzalez often capped his touchdown scores by dunking the football over the 10-foot-high goal post crossbar.

8 **Victor Cruz's Salsa Dance**
Despite going undrafted in 2010, Cruz burst onto the scene for the Giants in his second year, becoming quarterback Eli Manning's favorite target. During that season, he unveiled one of the most famous touchdown celebrations the league has ever seen. Honoring the memory of his grandmother, who taught him to dance, Cruz breaks into the traditional Latin dance after every score. That included the touchdown he scored in the Giants' Super Bowl XLVI victory.

10 **The Worm**
Johnnie Morton had only eight touchdown catches with the Kansas City Chiefs, but one of them prompted a TD celebration for the ages. After Morton caught a 28-yard touchdown pass during a 2003 game against the Cleveland Browns, he fell to the ground and performed the Worm, a move popularized by break-dancers in the 1980s. Morton slinked across the back of the end zone on his belly before jumping back onto his feet to celebrate with his teammates.

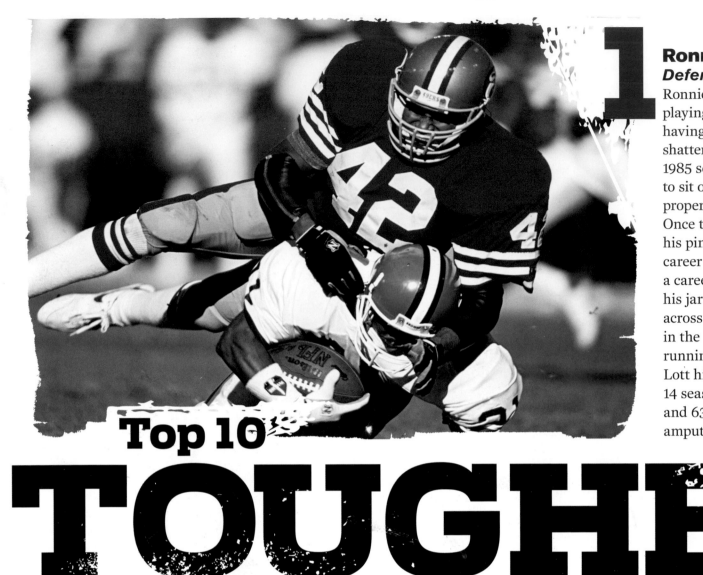

Ronnie Lott
Defensive Back (1981–94)

1

Ronnie Lott was so tough, he decided that playing football was more important than having all 10 of his fingers. When Lott shattered his left pinkie in the last week of the 1985 season, the San Francisco 49ers told him to sit out the playoffs so the finger could heal properly. Lott chose to play in pain instead. Once the season was over, Lott had the top of his pinkie cut off and played the rest of his career without a piece of the finger. And what a career it turned out to be. Best known for his jarring hits on anyone who dared to come across the middle of the field, Lott struck fear in the hearts of his opponents. Whether it was running backs, wide receivers, or quarterbacks, Lott hit them all and hit them hard. Over 14 seasons, Lott had four 100-tackle seasons and 63 career interceptions — and one amputated digit — in a Hall of Fame career.

Top 10
TOUGHEST

5

Emmitt Smith *Running Back (1990–2004)*
In the last game of the 1993 season, Emmitt Smith ran for 168 yards and helped the Dallas Cowboys clinch the NFC East — all while suffering from a separated right shoulder. That type of toughness was on display throughout Smith's 15-year career. The Hall of Fame running back played in 226 games, becoming the NFL's all-time rushing leader (18,355 yards).

Mean Joe Greene
Defensive Tackle (1969–81)
The man who was nicknamed Mean played in 181 of 190 possible games over the course of his career as one of the most intimidating defensive linemen ever. Mean Joe Greene was a two-time Defensive Player of the Year for the Pittsburgh Steelers. He played in four Super Bowls, six AFC title games, and 10 Pro Bowls. Greene's violent style could single-handedly influence games.

6

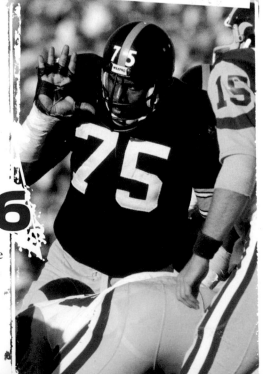

7

Bruce Matthews
Offensive Lineman (1983–2001)
No NFL offensive lineman has played in more games than Bruce Matthews (296). Over his 19-year career with the Houston Oilers and Tennessee Titans, he played at every position along the offensive line, starting 116 games at guard, 87 at center, and 39 at tackle.

Brett Favre
*Quarterback
(1991–2010)*
In the hard-hitting world of the NFL, 297 consecutive starts equals a whole lot of toughness. From September 27, 1992, through January 20, 2008, only one guy started under center for the Green Bay Packers. And Number 4 didn't stop there. When Brett Favre left the Packers, he kept going, first with the New York Jets and finally with the Minnesota Vikings. Despite a slew of injuries, Favre played the game's most important position for nearly 19 years without missing a start.

2

Walter Payton
*Running Back
(1975–87)*
The man they called Sweetness wasn't so sweet to opposing defensive backs. After missing one game in his rookie season with the Chicago Bears, Walter Payton went on to play the game's most physically demanding position for 184 consecutive games. At 5'10", 200 pounds, Payton wasn't the most imposing back, but that didn't stop him from regularly running over opposing defenders. The workhorse finished with 300 or more carries 10 times in his career. Despite the pounding he took, Sweetness finished with more than 21,000 all-purpose yards and won two MVP awards.

3

4

Jim Otto *Center (1960–74)*
The AFL lasted for 10 years, and Jim Otto played in every possible game in the league's history. Otto didn't just play, he starred, earning All-AFL honors 10 times. The center, who started in each of the Oakland Raiders' first 210 games, ruled the trenches as the leader of a talented O-line that helped Oakland win seven division championships and one AFL title.

PLAYERS

Jack Lambert
*Linebacker
(1971–84)*
Jack Lambert and his trademark toothless scowl served as the heart and soul of the Pittsburgh Steelers' famed Steel Curtain defense during the 1970s. In addition to making signature plays in both pass and run coverage, Lambert missed only seven games in his first 10 years in the league. The four-time Super Bowl winner was inducted into the Hall of Fame in 1990.

8

9

Jon Runyan *Tackle (1996–2009)*
Jon Runyan played in 207 games, starting 192 of them, and became one of the most feared O-linemen in the game. The 6'7" tackle played in every playoff contest for the Philadelphia Eagles during their run of four straight conference championship games from 2001 through 2004.

Jack Youngblood
*Defensive End
(1956–72)*
A relentless tackler, Jack Youngblood sat out only one game in 14 NFL seasons. That included the 1979 playoffs, when he broke his leg but still played every defensive down of the Los Angeles Rams' next two games, including the Super Bowl. Youngblood also played in seven straight Pro Bowls.

10

TOP MEN HAIR

1 Troy Polamalu
Safety

Troy Polamalu's long black curls are his trademark. It's no wonder his hair is insured for one million dollars and that he's a spokesman for Head & Shoulders (this photo was taken while filming one of the shampoo's commercials). His locks aren't always an asset, though. In 2006, the Pittsburgh Steelers safety was returning an interception against the Kansas City Chiefs when running back Larry Johnson pulled Polamalu down by his hair. Later, Polamalu joked that he wouldn't have to cut his hair because he'd "lost half of it already."

10 orable Styles

2 **Tom Brady**
Quarterback

In 2010, Tom Brady's hair was talked about almost as much as his play on the field was. After drawing comparisons to pop star Justin Bieber's famous 'do, Brady kept letting his hair grow shaggier and shaggier. By 2011, he was sporting a ponytail.

3 **Chad Ochocinco**
Wide Receiver

Chad Ochocinco debuted his golden Mohawk in training camp in 2006, but the colorful wide receiver promised to shave it if his Cincinnati Bengals lost a Week 8 game to the Atlanta Falcons. The Falcons won, and Ochocinco's bald dome was on display again.

4 **Tim Tebow**
Quarterback

The QB's teammates gave him a buzz-worthy new look prior to the 2010 season. As part of a rookie initiation, Denver Broncos linebacker Wesley Woodyard shaved the top of Tim Tebow's head, leaving only a ring of hair that looked like a doughnut.

5 **Randy Moss**
Wide Receiver

Already one of the league's taller receivers at 6' 4", Randy Moss's Afro during the 2004 season gave him an extra few inches. Moss and his hairdo had a lot in common: Both had plenty of volume and a larger-than-life presence.

6 **Brian Bosworth**
Linebacker

Brian Bosworth rocked the mullet with authority and lived up to the hairstyle's motto: business in the front, party in the back. The look ultimately outlived the linebacker's NFL career, which lasted only three seasons.

7 **Domata Peko**
Defensive Tackle

It's difficult to say who has a more difficult task: the offensive linemen whose job is to contain Domata Peko on the gridiron, or the Cincinnati Bengals helmet that has to contain Peko's long and fluffy mane of red hair.

8 **Larry Fitzgerald**
Wide Receiver

Larry Fitzgerald proudly sports long, thick dreadlocks in honor of his mother, Carol, who died in 2003 after battling cancer. She also wore her hair in dreads and liked the way they looked on the star Arizona Cardinals wide receiver.

9 **Clay Matthews**
Linebacker

Clay Matthews's long blonde locks have practically taken on a life of their own, especially online. The linebacker's hair has multiple Facebook fan pages. If his football career doesn't work out, he can always become a cover model for romance novels.

10 **Donovan McNabb**
Quarterback

While playing for the Philadelphia Eagles in 2004, Donovan McNabb was all smiles knowing that his hair would not spring unexpectedly into action during games — the quarterback kept it in neatly braided cornrows.

Top Run

1 Jim Brown
Cleveland Browns (1957–65)

For nine years, Jim Brown was the most dominant running back in the NFL, plowing over linemen while speeding to the goal line. Even if a defender latched on to him, he'd break free before reaching the end zone. "It's like tackling a locomotive," Los Angeles Rams defensive tackle Glenn Holtzman said about Brown in 1958. The durable bruiser was indeed always steaming ahead. In one of his last regular-season games, Brown tore through the Dallas Cowboys' defense after receiving a handoff in the second quarter. At the five-yard line, Cowboys linebacker Dave Edwards grabbed Brown's legs with both arms. Even then, Brown didn't give up. He forged ahead, pummeled through three more Dallas defenders and scored. A three-time MVP, Brown finished his career with 12,312 rushing yards, 262 receptions, and 15,459 combined net yards. The Hall of Famer played in nine straight Pro Bowls and never missed a single game in his career.

10
ning Backs

2 Walter Payton
Chicago Bears (1975–87)

On his way to 16,726 career rushing yards (second-most in NFL history), Walter Payton punished opposing teams with his relentless running style. He ran for 110 TDs and scored 15 more on receptions. Payton's combination of strength and grace left defenders in awe. During one game in 1985, with the Bears down 10–9 in the fourth quarter, Payton took the ball and ran into Green Bay Packers linebacker Brian Noble. "I knocked him back about four yards," Noble said, "but he stayed up and just kept going. Touchdown. Sitting in the locker room afterward, I was ready to quit. But my teammate John Anderson put his arm around me and said, 'Believe me, that's not the first time and it won't be the last time that Walter Payton breaks a tackle like that.'"

3 Emmitt Smith *Dallas Cowboys (1990–2002), Arizona Cardinals (2003–04)*

The NFL's all-time rushing leader was one of the most consistent producers the game has ever seen. Emmitt Smith went 11 straight seasons with at least 1,000 yards rushing. Smith, who finished his career with 18,355 yards, won four rushing crowns and led the league in rushing touchdowns three times. He was a key contributor to the Cowboys dynasty in the 1990s, helping the team win three Super Bowls in four years. Smith had more rushing touchdowns (164) and carried the ball more often (4,409 attempts) than any other running back in history. In postseason play he holds career records for rushing yards (1,586) and rushing touchdowns (19).

4 Barry Sanders *Detroit Lions (1989–98)*

There was no containing Barry Sanders. He zigzagged down the field and leaped over defenders, all while making it look effortless. With his video game moves, Sanders became the first player to rush for 1,000 yards in each of his first 10 seasons. In 1997 Sanders was named the league's MVP. That year he rushed for a league-leading 2,053 yards and gained another 305 yards on 33 catches. He also had more than 100 yards rushing for an NFL-record 14 consecutive regular-season games. Sanders likely would have made an even bigger mark in the record book had he not retired after the 1998 season, while still in his prime. He was inducted into the Pro Football Hall of Fame in 2004.

7 Marshall Faulk *Indianapolis Colts (1994–98), St. Louis Rams (1999–2005)*

Talk about a dual threat. The versatile Marshall Faulk, a 2011 Pro Football Hall of Fame inductee, wasn't only a dynamic rusher, he was also a game-breaking receiver. Tenth all-time on the career rushing list (12,279 yards), Faulk finished his career with 767 catches. Only four other Hall of Famers have caught more passes — three wide receivers and a tight end. The 2000 NFL MVP set the all-time record for receiving yards by a running back (6,875). Faulk is the only back to rush for at least 70 TDs and catch at least 30 touchdown passes. A three-time Offensive Player of the Year, he also helped the Rams win Super Bowl XXXIV.

8 Eric Dickerson *Los Angeles Rams (1983–87), Indianapolis Colts (1987–91), Los Angeles Raiders (1992), Atlanta Falcons (1993)*

Eric Dickerson's agility helped put him in the record book. In 1984 he rushed for an NFL-record 2,105 yards. Dickerson also holds the record for most yards in a playoff game, when he gained 248 yards against the Dallas Cowboys in 1985. Three years later, he became the seventh running back to rush for more than 10,000 yards, a milestone he reached faster than any other player (91 games). Dickerson had an electrifying running style that propelled him to the rushing title four times. By the time Dickerson retired in 1999, his swift feet had helped him become the NFL's second all-time leading rusher (13,259 yards on 2,996 carries).

5 Gale Sayers *Chicago Bears (1965–71)*

Gale Sayers knew how to make an entrance. In his rookie year, he scored 22 touchdowns, an NFL record for first-year players. Sayers didn't have a lengthy career, due to injuries, but his production during his seven seasons in the league was enough to make him an NFL great. He is tied for first for the most touchdowns scored in a game (six) and earned rushing titles in 1966 and 1969.

Sayers's toughness was remarkable. In the ninth game of the 1968 season, he injured his left knee, which required surgery. He fought hard to come back the following year. Sayers returned in 1969 and rushed for more than 1,000 yards. For his career, he had 9,435 combined net yards and 4,956 yards rushing.

6 Earl Campbell *Houston Oilers (1978–84), New Orleans Saints (1984–85)*

One hundred–yard rushing games are impressive, but 200-yard games are on a different level. In 1980, Earl Campbell broke the 200-yard mark in four games, an NFL record. He finished with a total of 1,934 yards that season and led the league in rushing for the third consecutive season. (Campbell won his first rushing title in 1978, becoming the first rookie to do so since 1957.)

Campbell sparked a turnaround for the Houston Oilers when he joined the team. Behind his fast and powerful runs, the Oilers ended an eight-year playoff drought and made back-to-back conference title games in 1978 and '79. Campbell was inducted into the Pro Football Hall of Fame in 1991.

9 Tony Dorsett *Dallas Cowboys (1977–87), Denver Broncos (1988)*

In one of the most memorable runs in NFL history, Tony Dorsett dashed to the end zone for a historic 99-yard touchdown against the Minnesota Vikings on January 3, 1983. The touchdown is the longest run from scrimmage in NFL history. It was one of many impressive plays that Dorsett made. He finished his career with 12,739 rushing yards and 91 touchdowns. No stranger

to the postseason, the Hall of Famer made two Super Bowl appearances and played in five NFC Championship Games. In 17 postseason games, Dorsett totaled 1,383 rushing yards and 1,786 yards from scrimmage. The four-time Pro Bowler is among the all-time scrimmage yards leaders, with 16,293.

10 LaDainian Tomlinson *San Diego Chargers (2001–09), New York Jets (2010–present)*

Emmitt Smith accomplished it in 160 games, but it took LaDainian Tomlinson only 137 matchups to reach 150 touchdowns, making him the fastest player to do so. Scoring seems to come naturally for Tomlinson, who holds the NFL single-season record for total touchdowns (31) and rushing TDs (28). In

2003, he became the first player in league history to rush for 1,000 yards and have 100 receptions in the same season. And Tomlinson can do more than just run and catch. In 2005, he became the seventh player in NFL history to run, catch, and throw for a touchdown, in a game against the Oakland Raiders.

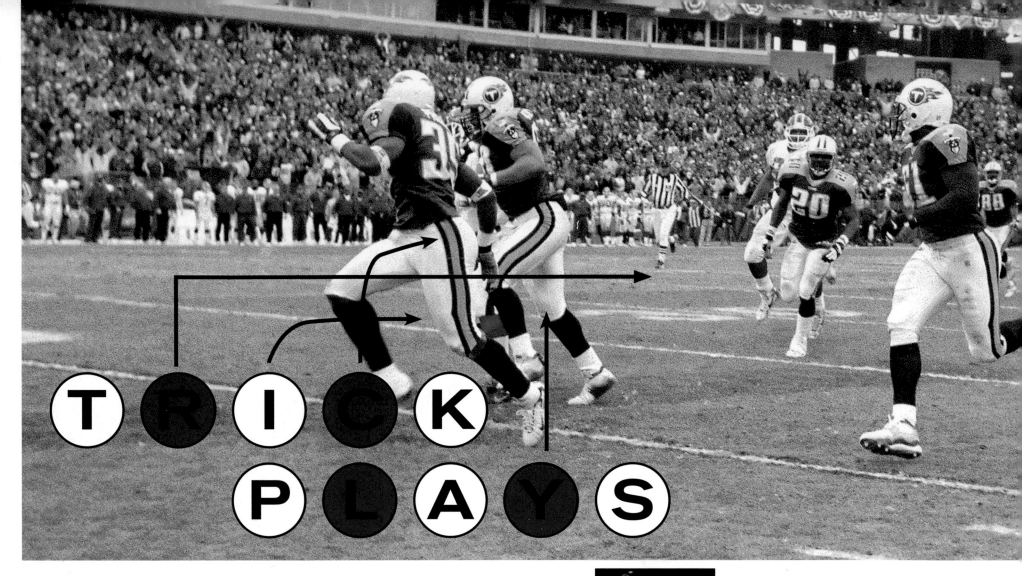

TRICK PLAYS

1 **The Tennessee Titans pull off the Music City Miracle**

▲ With their season 16 seconds away from coming to an end, the Tennessee Titans needed a miracle — and they got one. On January 8, 2000, in a Wild Card playoff game against the Buffalo Bills, Tennessee was down 16–15 and receiving the kickoff for its final drive of the game. Fullback Lorenzo Neal fielded the kick and quickly pitched it back to tight end Frank Wycheck, the Titans' leading receiver that day. Upon catching it, Wycheck ran a few steps and then threw it to Titans receiver Kevin Dyson, who found a seam down the left sideline. Dyson sprinted 75 yards for the game-winning score on a play that became known as the Music City Miracle. The Titans kept rolling in the playoffs that season, making it all the way to the Super Bowl.

2 **The New Orleans Saints recover an onside kick in Super Bowl XLIV**

New Orleans came out of halftime of Super Bowl XLIV trailing by four, ready to kick the ball off to the Indianapolis Colts. At least, that's what everybody thought. But Saints coach Sean Payton had a different idea. Payton took a huge gamble by asking punter Thomas Morstead to onside-kick the ball to the left side of the field. The Colts were caught off guard and flubbed the catch. The Saints recovered the ball near midfield, and six plays later, they had the lead. New Orleans went on to win its first Super Bowl in franchise history.

3 **Wide receiver Antwaan Randle El throws a touchdown pass to Hines Ward in Super Bowl XL**

◄ Leading 14–10 with less than 10 minutes to go in the fourth quarter, the Pittsburgh Steelers used a little bit of razzle dazzle to secure their franchise's fifth Super Bowl victory. On first and 10 from the Seattle Seahawks' 43-yard line, Pittsburgh QB Ben Roethlisberger pitched the ball back to Willie Parker, who handed it off to Antwaan

Randle El on a reverse. Randle El then threw a pass on the run to a streaking Hines Ward, who triumphantly skipped into the end zone for the final points of Super Bowl XL.

4 **Miami Dolphins QB Dan Marino pretends to spike the ball against the New York Jets**

◄ In a crucial road game against the division rival New York Jets in 1994, the Miami Dolphins had the ball at the Jets' eight-yard line with less than 30 seconds on the clock. Miami quarterback Dan Marino signaled for a spike to stop the clock. As the Jets' defense let up, Marino instead decided to throw the ball, finding Mark Ingram in the end zone for the game-winning score.

5 **The New Orleans Saints complete three laterals**

► Down by seven with seven seconds left and the ball at their own 25-yard line, the New Orleans Saints had one last chance in a game against the Jacksonville Jaguars during the 2003 season. Saints quarterback Aaron Brooks completed a pass along the right

sideline to Donte' Stallworth who, after weaving through the defense, lateraled to Michael Lewis. Lewis dropped the ball off to Deuce McAllister, who, in the midst of being tackled by a group of Jaguars defenders, launched a perfect cross-field lateral to Jerome Pathon, who ran in for the score. But the amazing 75-yard, three-lateral scoring play was for naught: Saints kicker John Carney missed the extra point, resulting in a one-point loss.

6 The Miami Dolphins pull off the first hook-and-ladder play

After falling behind 24–0 in the first quarter of their 1981 divisional playoff game against the San Diego Chargers, the Miami Dolphins cut the lead to 24–10. With six seconds to go in the half, Miami took a calculated risk and attempted the first hook-and-ladder play in NFL history. Dolphins QB Don Strock completed a pass to wideout Duriel Harris, who held on to the ball for a split second before lateraling to running back Tony Nathan. Nathan then scampered into the end zone, cutting the lead to seven. The Chargers won the seesaw battle, however, 41–38.

7 Tom Brady throws to Randy Moss; Moss tosses it back to Brady; Brady launches a touchdown pass to Jabar Gaffney

▶ With a four-point lead and the ball at their own 44-yard line in a 2007 game against the Pittsburgh Steelers, the New England Patriots' Tom Brady threw a quick lateral to Randy Moss. Moss threw a lateral back to Brady, who then turned downfield to find a wide open Jabar Gaffney in the end zone. Brady's 56-yard TD pass gave the Patriots a 24–13 lead in a game they went on to win 34–13.

8 Devin Hester catches a field goal and runs for a 108-yard TD

▼ Devin Hester is known for his kick returns, but a field goal return? Clinging to a 24–20 lead, the Chicago Bears sent Hester into the end zone during a fourth-quarter field-goal attempt by the New York Giants in 2006. Hester caught the missed kick eight yards deep in his own end zone and pretended as if he were going to down the ball. But after a split-second hesitation, he took off for the right sideline, racing for a 108-yard touchdown.

9 Randy Moss laterals to Moe Williams in a hook-and-ladder play

On the last play of the first half of a 7–7 game against the Denver Broncos during the 2003 season, Minnesota Vikings QB Daunte Culpepper lofted a 43-yard bomb to wideout Randy Moss. As Moss was being dragged down by two defenders, he acrobatically flipped the ball over his shoulder to a cutting Moe Williams, who took the ball into the end zone for a lead the Vikings would never lose.

10 John Carlson falls down, loses blocker, catches touchdown

▶ The Wild Card game of the 2010 playoffs between the Seattle Seahawks and the New Orleans Saints featured one truly wild play. On first-and-goal from the Saints' seven yard line, Seahawks tight end John Carlson pretended to fall down when the ball was snapped, which caused the Saints defenders to stop covering him. But Carlson quickly jumped back to his feet and ran into the end zone, where he caught a touchdown pass. His score helped the Seahawks knock off the defending Super Bowl champs.

Top 10
Football Players
Who Were Also Great In
Other Sports

1 Bo Jackson
Baseball

How do you balance careers in baseball and football? Bo knows. Bo Jackson is the greatest two-sport pro athlete of our time. Not only did he make the 1990 Pro Bowl as a running back, but he was also an All-Star outfielder in the majors. He won the All-Star MVP award in 1989.

6 Otto Graham
Basketball

Before he starred at quarterback for the Cleveland Browns, Otto Graham played college hoops at Northwestern and won the 1946 National Basketball League title with the Rochester Royals.

2 Jim Brown
Lacrosse
Whether Jim Brown had a football or a lacrosse stick in his hands, he was going to score. The Hall of Fame running back was a standout college lacrosse player, scoring 43 goals in 10 games as a senior at Syracuse.

3 Jim Thorpe
Track and Field, Baseball
Some call Jim Thorpe the greatest athlete in history. A Pro Football Hall of Famer, he also won gold medals in the pentathlon and decathlon at the 1912 Olympics and played six seasons of major league baseball.

4 Deion Sanders
Baseball
The swift cornerback proved to be a threat on the baseball diamond too. Deion Sanders was an outfielder for four major league teams. In 1994 he stole 38 bases, second-most in the National League.

5 Bob Hayes
Track and Field
Bob Hayes earned the title World's Fastest Man after winning gold medals in the 100 meters and 4×100-meter relay at the 1964 Summer Olympics. A year later, Hayes joined the Dallas Cowboys.

7 John Elway
Baseball
As a sophomore at Stanford, John Elway hit .361. He was drafted by the New York Yankees in 1981 but left baseball to play quarterback for the Denver Broncos in 1983.

8 Willie Gault
Track and Field
Willie Gault was not only a speedy wide receiver, he was also fast on the track. Gault was a member of the 4×100-meter relay team that won the 1983 world championship.

9 Julius Peppers
Basketball
A 6' 7" defensive end, Julius Peppers walked on to the University of North Carolina basketball team. He had 21 points and 10 rebounds in a 2001 NCAA tournament game.

10 Brian Jordan
Baseball
After three seasons as a safety, Brian Jordan left the NFL to play baseball full-time. The All-Star finished his 15-year major league career with a .282 batting average.

Top 10 Stadiums

AT&T Stadium

They say everything is bigger in Texas, and that's certainly the case with AT&T Stadium. In 2009, the Dallas Cowboys moved into the colossal state-of-the-art venue that seats 80,000 (and expanded to 100,000 seats for Super Bowl XLV). Not only does it have the largest retractable roof in the world, but it also features a truly jumbo Jumbotron that stretches from one 20-yard line to the other.

2 Soldier Field
Chicago Bears
Known for its iconic row of Greek columns, Soldier Field has been home to the Bears since 1971. The lake-front stadium is the smallest in the NFL and underwent a renovation in 2003 that brought fans even closer to the action.

3 Lambeau Field
Green Bay Packers
The oldest NFL stadium has had sellout crowds at every game since 1960. Lambeau hosted one of the most memorable games in NFL history: the 1967 championship, also known as the Ice Bowl, where temperatures reached –13°F.

4 Heinz Field
Pittsburgh Steelers
Named after the ketchup company, Heinz Field features replica bottles atop the scoreboard that simulate the pouring of the condiment onto the Jumbotron when the Steelers reach the red zone. The horseshoe design opens onto a scenic waterfront.

5 CenturyLink Field
Seattle Seahawks
With views of Mount Rainier and $2 million worth of art on display, CenturyLink Field is one of the most picturesque stadiums in the NFL. It's also one of the loudest, which is why false-start penalties are common among Seahawks opponents.

6 Sports Authority Field
Denver Broncos
After leaving Mile High Stadium following the 2000 season, the Broncos settled into a new home that features a 27-foot statue of Bucky the Bronco, Denver's mascot. And the stadium features 560 concession stands, so no fan leaves hungry.

7 Lucas Oil Stadium
Indianapolis Colts
Colts fans get a view of the Indianapolis skyline thanks to Lucas Oil Stadium's retractable six-panel window wall at the north end of the field. The stadium, which opened in 2008, also hosted the NCAA men's basketball Final Four in 2010 and '15.

8 Arrowhead Stadium
Kansas City Chiefs
When Arrowhead opened in 1972, Chicago Bears coach George Halas called it "the most revolutionary, futuristic sports complex I have ever seen." The reputation remains true, thanks in part to a $375 million renovation that was completed in 2010.

9 Ralph Wilson Stadium
Buffalo Bills
If you're going to a game at the open-air Ralph Wilson Stadium, hold on to your hat. Buffalo is already a windy city, but the stadium's design (the field sits 50 feet below ground level), means even more blustery conditions — and a cool view.

10 Ford Field
Detroit Lions
When Ford Field opened in 2002, it was the first time since 1975 that the Lions had played within Detroit's city limits. (Their old stadium was about 30 miles away.) Even though it's an indoor facility, skylights and windows allow the sun to shine in.

1 Deion Sanders
Cornerback (1989–2005)

Comedian Denis Leary once said in a commercial that Deion Sanders had about 27 nicknames. That's not quite true — he was known as Prime Time and Neon Deion — but if anyone had the personality to fit 27 nicknames, it was Sanders. He took showboating to a whole new level, high-stepping into the end zone and performing elaborate celebration dances. He even released a rap album in 1994.

2 Tim Rossovich
Linebacker (1968–76)

Don't try Tim Rossovich's antics at home. As a joke, he once showed up to a friend's party after lighting himself on fire. He was also known for chewing glass.

3 John Randle
Defensive Tackle (1990–2003)

It took guts just to look John Randle in the eyes. The Hall of Famer wore smeared eye black to intimidate opponents. He was also a relentless trash-talker.

Top 10 Colorful

8 Richard Sherman
Cornerback
(2011–present)

Sherman is the outspoken leader of Seattle's "Legion of Boom" secondary. He's brash and bright: He had a perfect grade-point average in high school and attended Stanford, one of the nation's top schools.

4 **Joe Namath**
Quarterback (1965–77)
Broadway Joe Namath never shied from the bright lights of New York City. He showed off his sense of style and was known for his long sideburns and flashy fur coats. One of the most famous commercials in history starred Namath, showing off his legs in an ad for women's pantyhose.

5 **Clinton Portis**
Running Back (2002–10)
For football players, weekly interviews with reporters can be boring. To liven things up, Clinton Portis started appearing in outrageous costumes. The Pro Bowler's characters included Sheriff Gonna Getcha, Coach Janky Spanky, Southeast Jerome, and Choo Choo.

6 **Jim McMahon**
Quarterback (1982–96)
Jim McMahon was perfect as the face of the Chicago Bears in the 1980s: confident, fun, and in your face. His headbands, wild haircuts, and dark sunglasses were trademark looks. McMahon was sometimes referred to as an offensive lineman in a quarterback's body.

7 **Brian Bosworth**
Linebacker (1987–89)
The linebacker's pro career lasted little more than two seasons, but Brian Bosworth made plenty of waves in that short time, sporting a blond mullet and trash-talking to the media. After his NFL career ended, the Boz took his act to Hollywood, starring in action films.

Personalities

9 **Chad Johnson**
Wide Receiver (2001–12)
It doesn't get much wackier than changing your name to match your uniform number, but for a few years Chad Johnson was legally known as Chad Ochocinco. An avid end zone dancer, Johnson was a natural choice to compete on *Dancing With the Stars*.

10 **Terrell Owens**
Wide Receiver (1996–2012)
Terrell Owens's brash personality clashed with his quarterbacks and earned him his own reality-TV show. He also set a new standard for TD celebrations in 2002, when he pulled out a pen from his sock and autographed the ball.

1

Deacon Jones
Defensive End (1961–74)

During the playing career of Deacon Jones (number 75), the NFL did not track sacks as a statistic. So in 2008, the magazine *Pro Football Weekly* re-watched his game film to calculate just how many sacks Jones had. They approximated "The Secretary of Defense" had three seasons of 20 or more sacks for the Los Angeles Rams. Since the NFL started tracking sacks in 1982, there have been only 11 20-sack seasons. Jones's numbers are even more impressive when you consider that not only were NFL seasons just 14 games at the time, but teams didn't try to pass nearly as often as they do today, meaning fewer chances for sacks.

Top 10
Sack Mast

2 Reggie White
Defensive End (1985–2000)

"The Minister of Defense," had a rare blend of power and quickness. He had up 10 or more sacks in each of his first nine seasons, dominating for the Eagles and later the Packers.

3 Bruce Smith
Defensive End (1985–2003)

Smith is the only man in NFL history to record 200 career sacks. He was the heart of a Buffalo Bills defense that went to four consecutive Super Bowls in the 1990s.

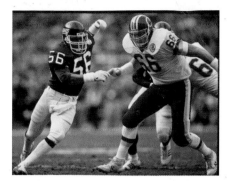

4 Lawrence Taylor
Linebacker (1981–93)

Taylor had 20.5 sacks for the Super Bowl champion 1986 Giants. The explosive edge rusher is the only player to be named AP Defensive Player of the Year three times.

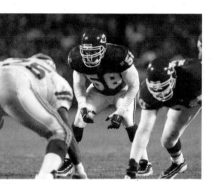

5 Derrick Thomas
Linebacker (1989–99)

A nine-time Pro Bowler, Thomas had one of the greatest games ever. On Nov. 11, 1990, he recorded seven sacks against the Seahawks, still a single-game record.

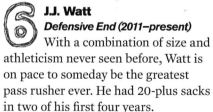

6 J.J. Watt
Defensive End (2011–present)

With a combination of size and athleticism never seen before, Watt is on pace to someday be the greatest pass rusher ever. He had 20-plus sacks in two of his first four years.

7 Gino Marchetti
Defensive End (1952–66)

The seven-time All-Pro played offensive line early in his career. It helped him learn to beat blockers. He led the D on a Colts team that won back-to-back titles in 1958 and '59.

8 DeMarcus Ware
Linebacker (2005–present)

A four-time All-Pro with the Cowboys, Ware tied an NFL record by recording a sack in 10 straight games between 2007 and '08. He's still terrorizing QBs now, for Denver.

9 Doug Atkins
Defensive End (1953–69)

At 6' 8", Atkins was a monstrous presence on the Chicago Bears' defensive line. Overpowering blockers, he made the Pro Bowl eight times in his 12 seasons with the Bears.

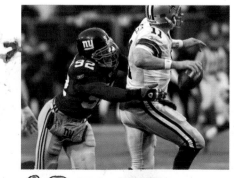

10 Michael Strahan
Defensive End (1993–2007)

Strahan holds the single-season sack record, 22 ½ in 2001. He ended his career in style, with a sack of Tom Brady to help the Giants win Super Bowl XLII, his final game.

1 LaDainian Tomlinson's visor

Running back LaDainian Tomlinson is the man behind the mask. But the dark visor is more than just a way to intimidate opponents. When he played at Texas Christian University, a doctor recommended that Tomlinson wear the tinted visor to help stop the migraine headaches he was suffering because he was sensitive to light. The visor quickly became a vital part of his game-day gear, although Tomlinson admits he also likes the way it looks. "If you pay attention to the photos of players, their eyes are all big," says Tomlinson. "I never liked those shots. When we were kids, one of my best friends used to always make fun of people. He'd say, 'Ooh, I wonder what that guy's thinking,' and make funny jokes. I hated that."

TOP 10

ACCESSORIES

2 Jim McMahon's headband

Jim McMahon's headband did more than mop up sweat. It doubled as a billboard. In 1986, after NFL commissioner Pete Rozzelle fined the Chicago Bears quarterback $5,000 for wearing a headband with a corporate logo, McMahon protested by scrawling ROZELLE on his headband the next week.

3 Johnny Unitas's high-tops

San Diego Chargers defensive tackle Dave Costa once called Johnny Unitas "the chairman of the board of the high-top society." Unitas, who played in the NFL for 18 seasons, wore the trademark shoes until his final game in 1973.

4 Bryan Cox's neck plate

After a severe neck injury during his rookie season in 1991, three-time Pro Bowler Bryan Cox began wearing an extended neck plate for more support and protection. The large pad made the hulking Cox look even more imposing on the field.

5 Breast cancer awareness gear

NFL players think pink in October. Since 2009, they've honored National Breast Cancer Awareness Month by wearing pink gear, including cleats, wristbands, gloves, and chin straps.

6 Ed McCaffrey's shoulder pads

Ed McCaffrey wore undersized shoulder pads so that he would be lighter and faster on the field. But it also meant that the wide receiver had less protection. "I've tried to take his pads from him, because they're right on the borderline of safety," Broncos equipment manager Doug West said in 1998, "but he won't let me."

7 Eric Dickerson's goggles

Poor vision didn't slow down Hall of Fame running back Eric Dickerson. In 1984, while wearing prescription goggles, he had a historic season, carrying the ball 379 times for 2,105 yards, an NFL record.

8 Deion Sanders's bandana

Deion Sanders wore a signature bandana under his helmet, but he had to give up the look later in his career. In 2001, the NFL declared that players could no longer wear bandanas or do-rags.

9 Terrell Owens's Sharpie

With the help of a Sharpie permanent marker, Terrell Owens created one of the most memorable touchdown celebrations ever. In a 2002 game against the Seattle Seahawks, Owens reached the end zone, then pulled a Sharpie out of his sock and autographed the ball for a fan.

10 Rich Karlis's bare foot

No shoe, no problem. In seven NFL seasons, placekicker Rich Karlis booted all of his field goals and extra points with his bare right foot. In the 1986 AFC Championship Game, Karlis made two barefooted field goals for the Denver Broncos even though the temperature was barely above freezing.

Ryan Leaf *Quarterback*

Draft 1998   **Overall Pick** Number 2   **Team** San Diego Chargers

Heading into the 1998 NFL Draft, some scouts thought Ryan Leaf was a better pick than Peyton Manning. Leaf was coming off a 10–2 season with Washington State, leading the Cougars to the Rose Bowl and throwing for nearly 4,000 yards and 34 touchdowns. Manning was taken Number 1, but Leaf went next. That was the highlight of Leaf's NFL career. As a rookie, he threw 15 interceptions and two touchdown passes while going 3–7 with the Chargers. In his three-season career, Leaf made 21 starts and threw more than twice as many picks as touchdowns.

2 JaMarcus Russell *Quarterback*

Draft 2007
Overall Pick Number 1
Team Oakland Raiders

The Raiders were enticed by JaMarcus Russell's impressive size (6' 6", 260 pounds) and strength. In three NFL seasons, however, he won only seven games, and Oakland released him after 2009.

3 Charles Rogers *Wide Receiver*

Draft 2003
Overall Pick Number 2
Team Detroit Lions

While at Michigan State, Charles Rogers broke Randy Moss's NCAA record for consecutive games with a touchdown catch (14). In the NFL, Rogers caught 36 passes in three seasons before falling out of the league.

4 Tim Couch *Quarterback*

Draft 1999
Overall Pick Number 1
Team Cleveland Browns

A Heisman Trophy finalist, Tim Couch was drafted ahead of Donovan McNabb, Edgerrin James, and Torry Holt. Couch never won more than eight games in any of his five NFL seasons.

TOP 10 DRAFT BUSTS

5 Akili Smith *Quarterback*

Draft 1999
Overall Pick Number 3
Team Cincinnati Bengals

When the Bengals drafted Akili Smith as their quarterback of the future out of Oregon, they were probably expecting more than his five career touchdown passes.

6 Tony Mandarich *Tackle-Guard*

Draft 1989
Overall Pick Number 2
Team Green Bay Packers

Tony Mandarich appeared on the cover of Sports Illustrated as "The Best Offensive Line Prospect Ever." He was cut by the Packers after three lackluster seasons.

7 Ki-Jana Carter *Running Back*

Draft 1995
Overall Pick Number 1
Team Cincinnati Bengals

As a rookie, Carter suffered a major knee injury during the preseason. He never fully recovered, as his 464 yards in 1997 ended up being the highest total of his career.

8 Heath Shuler *Quarterback*

Draft 1994
Overall Pick Number 3
Team Washington Redskins

After setting passing records in college at Tennessee, Heath Shuler threw 14 interceptions in 13 starts for Washington. He didn't fare any better with the Saints in 1997 (14 picks in 10 games).

9 Blair Thomas *Running Back*

Draft 1990
Overall Pick Number 2
Team New York Jets

An All-America at Penn State, Blair Thomas was taken 15 slots ahead of the NFL's all-time rushing leader, Emmitt Smith, and produced one eighth of Smith's career rushing yardage (2,236).

10 Steve Emtman *Defensive End*

Draft 1992
Overall Pick Number 1
Team Indianapolis Colts

Steve Emtman was the Pac-10 Defensive Player of the Year at Washington in 1991. But the Colts got only three seasons and five sacks out of their top pick, who badly injured both knees.

Top 10
Come

backs

1 Buffalo Bills 41 Houston Oilers 38

January 3, 1993

After Oilers defensive back Bubba McDowell returned an interception for a touchdown early in the third quarter of their AFC Wild Card playoff game against the Bills, Houston took a 35–3 lead that seemed impossible to overcome. To make matters worse, Bills star quarterback Jim Kelly was out with an injury, leaving backup Frank Reich to lead the offense. Reich did a masterful job, leading five touchdown drives in a 21-minute span to give the Bills the lead. But Houston scored a last-second field goal to force overtime. In OT, Buffalo defensive back Nate Odomes intercepted a pass on the first drive to set up Steve Christie's game-winning, 32-yard field goal. The biggest comeback win in NFL history was complete, and Buffalo was on its way to its third-straight Super Bowl.

2 San Francisco 49ers 38
New Orleans Saints 35
December 7, 1980

Hall of Fame quarterback Joe Montana was known for his amazing comebacks. His first one in the NFL came against the Saints. New Orleans entered the game winless, but the 49ers hadn't performed much better, going 4–28 over the previous two seasons. The Saints dominated the first half, outgaining the Niners in yardage 324 to 21 to jump out to a 35–7 halftime lead. That's when Montana, making his sixth career start, went to work. He led four touchdown drives in the second half, running for one TD and throwing for two others, to force overtime. San Francisco won the game on a field goal by Ray Wersching. The comeback helped launch the 49ers dynasty of the 1980s. One year later, the team won its first of four Super Bowls in that decade.

3 Indianapolis Colts 38
Tampa Bay Buccaneers 35
October 6, 2003

▼ It wasn't just that Peyton Manning and the Colts were down by three touchdowns with five minutes to go: They were trailing on the road, on *Monday Night Football*, and facing the defending Super Bowl–champion Bucs, who had one of the most dominant defenses in the NFL. That made no difference to Manning. The Colts scored a quick touchdown thanks to Brad Pyatt's 90-yard kickoff return, and then recovered an onside kick. That's when Manning took over. Six plays later, he connected with Marvin Harrison for a touchdown on fourth down. Then, after the Colts got the ball back with 1:41 left, Manning drove the Colts 85 yards down the field for the tying TD. In overtime, he engineered a 76-yard drive to set up Mike Vanderjagt's winning field goal. "It's the old cliche: 60 minutes," Manning said after the game. "Sometimes it's hard to keep believing that." The victory was especially sweet for Colts head coach Tony Dungy, who had been fired by Tampa two years earlier.

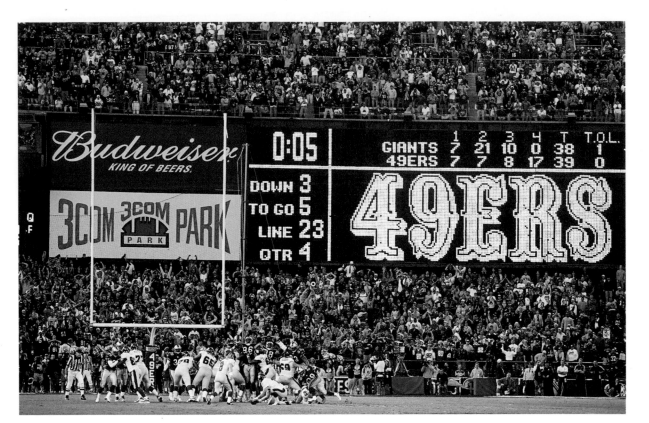

4 San Francisco 49ers 39
New York Giants 38
January 5, 2003

▲ With less than five minutes left in the third quarter of a Wild Card playoff game, the Giants had stretched their lead to 38–14. Niners fans were used to seeing star quarterbacks Joe Montana and Steve Young lead their team to victory, but this day they'd have to rely on Jeff Garcia, who had never won a playoff game. But Garcia delivered in his second postseason start. He threw a 26-yard TD pass to Terrell Owens late in the third quarter, then ran for a 14-yard score just two minutes later. A field goal cut the lead to five. With three minutes left, Garcia led a two-minute touchdown drive, finding Tai Streets in the end zone to give San Francisco a 39–38 lead. It wasn't over yet, though: The Giants lined up for a 40-yard field goal that would have won it, but a bad snap sealed the win for the Niners.

5 Dallas Cowboys 30
San Francisco 49ers 28
December 23, 1972

Cowboys quarterback Roger Staubach could only watch as his team fell behind 28–13 in their divisional playoff game. Staubach was out with a separated shoulder suffered in Week 5, but Dallas coach Tom Landry, desperate for the win, put his injured star back into the game as the fourth quarter began. Captain Comeback then delivered one of the most clutch performances in playoff history, throwing for 174 yards in the final quarter. Staubach's TD pass to Billy Parks with 1:20 left made it a one-score game. Dallas then recovered a clever onside kick (Toni Fritsch lined up to kick it left but instead flicked it to the right). That was the opening Staubach needed. He completed a game-winning TD to Ron Sellers in the final moments to send Dallas to the NFC title game.

6 Detroit Lions 31
San Francisco 49ers 27
December 22, 1957

When San Francisco took a 24–7 lead into halftime of their 1957 Western Conference title game with Detroit, the Niners seemed to have a trip to the NFL title game locked up. The team was so confident that it began printing tickets for the following week's game. That's when the Lions turned to the Bomb. Running back Tom (the Bomb) Tracy hadn't had a carry in the previous four games but was on the field as an injury replacement. Tracy ran for two third-quarter touchdowns that helped open up the Lions' offense. Quarterback Tobin Rote then directed two fourth-quarter scoring drives to give the Lions a 31–27 victory. A week later, Detroit beat Cleveland for its fourth NFL title.

7 New York Jets 40 Miami Dolphins 37
October 23, 2000

▶ This comeback had it all: a heated rivalry on *Monday Night Football*, first place on the line, and a touchdown catch by a guy named Jumbo. Miami was in control after three quarters, leading 30–7. Then Vinny Testaverde, New York's 36-year-old quarterback, began a fourth-quarter charge. He threw two touchdown passes and led another drive that ended in a field goal. With less than four minutes to go, he hit Wayne Chrebet for a 24-yard TD to tie the game. But the celebration was short-lived: On the next play from scrimmage, Miami's Jay Fiedler threw a 46-yard TD pass. Testaverde came right back, and with 42 seconds left he threw a play-action TD to offensive tackle Jumbo Elliott, who lined up as a tight end on the play. It was the only catch of Elliott's 14-season NFL career. Things were just as wacky in OT. Jets defensive back Marcus Coleman intercepted Fiedler, only to fumble the ball. Five plays later Coleman picked off Fiedler again, but held on to the ball this time. That allowed Testaverde to guide the offense and set up John Hall's game-winning field goal.

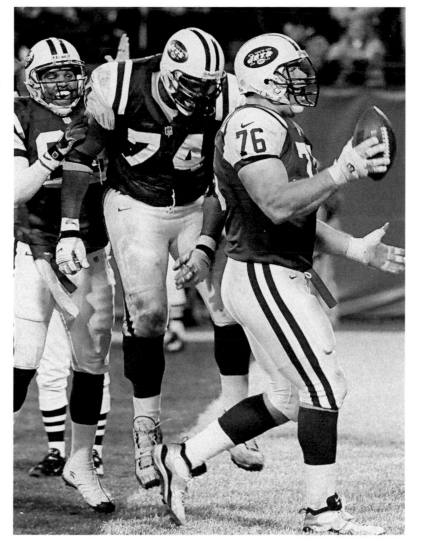

9 New England Patriots 34 Denver Broncos 31
November 24, 2013

Tom Brady vs. Peyton Manning might be the greatest quarterback rivalry of all time. Entering this game, Manning had won only two of his eight career games against Brady at New England. But it looked like he'd get a third win as the Broncos took a 24–0 lead at halftime on a cold and windy Sunday night. Not so fast. Brady came out on fire, leading touchdown drives on the first four possessions of the second half while the Patriots' defense shut down Denver. The Broncos needed a late touchdown just to force overtime. The game seemed headed for a tie as neither offense could move the ball in OT. That's when the Pats caught a break, as the Broncos muffed a punt to set up kicker Stephen Gostkowski's game-winning kick with less than two minutes left.

10 Cleveland Browns 29 Tennessee Titans 28
October 5, 2014

▼ It's hard to win on the road in the NFL. It's even harder when you fall behind by 25 points in the first half, as the Browns did at Tennessee, 28–3, in this game. Cleveland's quarterback, Brian Hoyer, was a journeyman who had never been more than a backup before becoming the Browns' starter in 2014. But he had already led two game-winning drives in the final two minutes of games that season. Hoyer proved to be a late-game hero in this one as well, throwing a touchdown at the end of the first half and two more in the fourth quarter (the Browns also got a field goal and a safety in the second half). The last TD came with just 1:09 left, giving the Browns their first lead of the game. When the Cleveland defense stuffed the Titans' desperation drive, it capped off the biggest comeback ever by a road team in the NFL.

8 Indianapolis Colts 45 Kansas City Chiefs 44
January 4, 2014

◄ The Colts' future was bright with Andrew Luck under center. But in this Wild-Card playoff game, it looked like they were doomed when the Chiefs took a 38–10 lead early in the third quarter. That's when Luck went to work. The young QB led two quick TD drives to make it 38–24. The Chiefs kicked a field goal to stretch their lead, but Luck countered with two more touchdown drives. The second one ended when running back Donald Brown fumbled at the goal line; the ball bounced back to Luck, who scooped it and dove for the TD. After another K.C. field goal made it a six-point game, Luck found speedster T.Y. Hilton for a 64-yard TD that proved to be the game-winner, capping the second-biggest comeback in NFL playoff history.

"Top 10 Quotes"

2
"We're going to win Sunday. I guarantee you."
—**Joe Namath,** New York Jets quarterback, predicting the outcome of his team's game against the heavily favored Baltimore Colts in Super Bowl III

3
"If my mother put on a helmet and shoulder pads and a uniform that wasn't the same as the one I was wearing, I'd run over her if she was in my way. And I love my mother."
—**Bo Jackson,** Los Angeles Raiders running back, on his competitive spirit

4
"I've been big ever since I was little."
—**William Perry,** Chicago Bears defensive tackle, on his size

5
"I feel like I'm the best, but you're not going to get me to say that."
—**Jerry Rice,** San Francisco 49ers wide receiver, explaining his worth while looking for a new contract

6
"Most football teams are temperamental. That's 90 percent temper and 10 percent mental."
—**Doug Plank,** Chicago Bears safety, explaining the personalities in the NFL

1

"Winning isn't everything, but it's the only thing. In our business, there is no second place. Either you're first or you're last."

—**Vince Lombardi,** Green Bay Packers coach, in a speech welcoming his players to the team

8

"You don't have to win it; just don't lose it."

—**Ray Lewis,** Baltimore Ravens linebacker, giving advice to QB Elvis Grbac prior to the 2001 season

7

"Sure, luck means a lot in football. Not having a good quarterback is bad luck."

—**Don Shula,** Miami Dolphins coach, on the importance of having a talented QB

10

"Pressure is something you feel when you don't know what you're doing."

—**Peyton Manning,** Indianapolis Colts quarterback, on the importance of preparation (inspired from a line by Hall of Fame coach Chuck Noll)

9

"The thing I like about football is that you don't have to take a shower before you go to work."

—**Jay Hilgenberg,** Chicago Bears center, on a perk of his job

TOP 10
FANS

1

Indianapolis Colts

The Colts' faithful bleed blue and are not afraid to let everyone know. In a home game against the Pittsburgh Steelers in 2005, the noise level in the RCA Dome reached 102 decibels. To get a sense of how loud that is, imagine a jackhammer pounding away 6½ feet from your ears. The fans have a way of getting in the heads of Colts opponents. "By no means am I excited to go play in Indianapolis," Steelers QB Ben Roethlisberger said about a rematch later that season.

MIKES
MASKED MANIACS

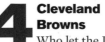

2 **Pittsburgh Steelers**
Famous for waving black-and-gold Terrible Towels, Steeler Nation is rooted in tradition and continues to be one of the most devoted fan bases in the league. Steelers fans even support their team on the road. In October 2008, Pittsburgh fans made up about 25 percent of the crowd at a Steelers-Jaguars game in Jacksonville, Florida.

3 **Green Bay Packers**
Thanks to the support of the Cheeseheads, the Packers have sold out every game at Lambeau Field since 1960.

4 **Cleveland Browns**
Who let the Dawgs out? The Dawg Pound behind the end zone in Cleveland Browns Stadium is one of the rowdiest sections in the NFL.

5 **Oakland Raiders**
With die-hard Raiders fans wearing skulls and spikes to scare off opponents, the Black Hole of Oakland Coliseum is loud and frightening.

6 **Washington Redskins**
The Hogettes put on dresses, hats, and pig snouts (a nod to the Hogs, the nickname for the Redskins' offensive lines of the 1980s).

7 **Minnesota Vikings**
The Vikings' fierce fans conquer the stands. Inspired by Minnesota's Nordic roots, they don Viking horns and yellow braids.

8 **Kansas City Chiefs**
Proud K.C. fans pack Arrowhead Stadium and give the Chiefs one of the biggest home-field advantages in the league.

9 **New Orleans Saints**
New Orleans's supporters are always rocking and rolling, especially when Elvis impersonators get the crowd all shook up.

10 **Philadelphia Eagles**
The Eagles know that they have to perform; otherwise, their intense fans will be quick to release the boo birds.

Photo Credits

Cover: Bill Frakes (10-yard line); Annmarie Avila (football)
Back Cover: Eric Christian Smith/AP (Watt); David N. Berkwitz (helmet); David E. Klutho (Brady, Polamalu); Peter Read Miller (Rice)
Title Page: John Biever
Copyright Page: Robert Beck
Table of Contents: Wesley Hitt/WireImage.com (5)
Rivalries: Doug Pensinger/Getty Images (Bears–Packers); Heinz Kluetmeier (Cowboys–Redskins); David Bergman (Colts–Patriots); Damian Strohmeyer (Giants–Eagles); John Biever (Ravens–Steelers, Packers–Vikings); Walter Iooss Jr. (Cowboys–49ers); Bill Frakes (Dolphins–Jets); John W. McDonough (Chiefs–Raiders); Peter Read Miller (Broncos–Chargers)
Quarterbacks: Richard Mackson (Montana, Elway); David E. Klutho (Brady, Rodgers); Walter Iooss Jr. (Unitas, Starr); Bill Frakes (Marino); Dustin Bradford/Getty Images (Manning); Morry Gash/AP (Favre); MPS/WireImage/Getty Images (Young)
Play Innovations: Peter Read Miller
Nicknames: Bill Smith/WireImage (Perry); John Biever (Bettis); TSN/Zuma Press/Icon SMI (Hirsch); George Lange (Sanders); John Iacono (Payton); World Wide Photos/AP (Lane); James Drake (Namath); Aaron Ontiveroz/The Denver Post/Getty Images (Johnson); Walter Iooss Jr. (Greene); Andy Hayt (Montana)
Helmets: David N. Berkwitz (10)
Touchdown Leaders: Peter Read Miller (Rice, Tomlinson, Owens, Faulk); Al Tielemans (Smith); John Iacono (Moss); Richard Mackson (Allen); Mickey Pfleger (Carter); Bob Rosato (Harrison); Neil Leifer (Brown)
Pro Football Movies: Getty Images (popcorn box); Walt Disney Pictures/Photofest (*Invincible*); Everett Collection (*Paper Lion*); © Paramount/Everett Collection (*The Longest Yard*)
Super Bowls: Heinz Kluetmeier (XLII); Walter Iooss Jr. (III); Mark Cowan/Icon SMI (XXXIV); Ronald C. Modra (XXV); Al Tielemans (XLIII); John Biever (XXIII, XXXVI); Robert Beck (XXXVIII); Focus on Sport/Getty Images (XLIX); John Iacono (X)
Fastest Players: Kevin Reece/Icon SMI (Johnson); James Drake/WireImage (Sanders); James Drake (Hayes); Peter Read Miller (Jackson); Shawn Thew/AFP/Getty Images (Green); Greg Ashman/Cal Sport Media (Moss); MPS/WireImage (Gault); G. Newman Lowrance/Getty Images (Hester); Rob Brown/WireImage (Branch, Brown)
Fantasy Performers: John W. McDonough (Faulk, Manning); Heinz Kluetmeier (Holmes); John Iacono (Brady); Peter Read Miller (Tomlinson); John Biever (Rice, Culpepper, Manning); Al Tielemans (Moss); Damian Strohmeyer (Gronkowski); Damian Strohmeyer (Ravens)
Unbreakable Records: AP
Big Guys: Courtesy of the Dallas Cowboys (Jones); WD/Icon SMI (Pace); Damian Strohmeyer (Bettis); Bob Rosato (Ogden); Al Tielemans (Jenkins, Wilfork); Fred Vuich (Hampton); David Stluka/Icon SMI (Brown); Scott Boehm/Getty Images (Gibson); Wesley Hitt/Getty Images (Davis)
Little Guys: Glenn James/WireImage (Barry Sanders); Bob Rosato (Brees); Doug Pensinger/Getty Images (Green); US Presswire (Mills); Streeter Lecka/Getty Images (Smith); Fernando Medina/US Presswire (Jones-Drew); Greg Nelson (Bob Sanders); Rick Stewart/Getty Images (Welker); UPI/Bettmann/Corbis (Young); Al Messerschmidt/WireImage (Flutie)
Wacky Weather: Heinz Kluetmeier (Eagles–Bears); Vernon Biever/Getty Images (Cowboys–Packers); Press-Gazette Archives (Bucs–Packers); Hugh Jones/Getty Images (Chiefs–Bucs); Fred Waters/AP (Giants–Cardinals); AP (Eagles–Cardinals, Chargers–Bengals); Mike Kullen/AP (Dolphins–Patriots); Brian Bahr/Getty Images (Packers–Cardinals); John Iacono (Raiders–Patriots)
Artifacts: Courtesy of the Pro Football Hall of Fame (9); David N. Berkwitz (ring)
Lovable Losers: Rebecca Cook/Reuters (Lions fan); Richard Mackson (Browns); Heinz Kluetmeier (Buccaneers); Doug Benc/Getty Images (Cardinals)
Undrafted Players: Simon Bruty (Warner, Romo); Anthony Neste (Moon); John Biever (Harrison); Heinz Kluetmeier (Randle); Tony Tomsic/Getty Images (Little); Bob Rosato (Gates, Holmes); Al Tielemans (Peters); Jeff Moffett/Icon SMI (Waters)
Passer-Receiver Duos: Greg Trott/AP (Montana and Rice); Brad Mangin (Young); Peter Read Miller (Rice, Aikman, Biletnikoff); Al Messerschmidt/WireImage.com (Bradshaw); NFL/WireImage.com (Swann); Walter Iooss Jr. (Unitas); Darryl Norenberg/WireImage.com (Berry); John Biever (Irvin); Focus on Sport/Getty Images (Stabler); Damian Strohmeyer (Manning); Bob Rosato (Harrison); Heinz Kluetmeier (Brady); Bill Frakes (Moss); Marc Serota/Reuters (Marino); Lonnie Major/Getty Images (Clayton); David E. Klutho (Culpepper); Al Tielemans (Moss)
Coaches: Neil Leifer (Lombardi); Al Tielemans (Shula); Bettmann/Corbis (Brown); Rich Clarkson (Noll); Damian Strohmeyer (Belichick); Robert Beck (Gibbs); John F. Jaqua (Halas); Walter Iooss Jr. (Landry); Bob Rosato (Parcells); AP (Lambeau)
Technical Innovations: David Bergman (instant replay); Brad Mangin (face mask); Greg Nelson (Jumbotron); David E. Klutho (Manning); Brian D. Kersey/Getty Images (tablet)
Football Families: Sporting News/Icon SMI (Mannings); Joe Robbins/Getty Images (Bruce Matthews, Kyle Long); NFL/WireImage.com (Clay Matthews Jr., Sterling Sharpe, Reed); Al Pereira/New York Jets/Getty Images (Clay Matthews III); Al Messerschmidt/Getty Images (Winslow Sr.); Gary Bogdon (Winslow II); Larry Busacca/WireImage (Shannon Sharpe); Manuello Paganelli (Barbers); Rob Carr/Getty Images (Harbaughs); Allen Dean Steele/WireImage.com (Randall Cunningham); Focus on Sport/Getty Images (Sam Cunningham); NCAA Photos (Carter); Taylor Hill/Filmmagic (Howie Long); Michael Thomas/Getty Images (Chris Long); Larry Marano/Getty Images for Tide (Davises)
Touchdown Celebrations: John Biever (Lambeau Leap); Peter Read Miller (Ickey Shuffle); Ronald C. Modra (Fun Bunch); Richard Mackson (Mile High Salute); Paul Sakuma/AP (Finger Roll); John Bazemore/AP (Dirty Bird); Michael Hickey/WireImage.com (Ochocinco); Wesley Hitt/Getty Images (Cruz); Scott D. Weaver/Icon SMI (Gonzalez); Wesley Hitt/WireImage.com (Worm, 4)
Toughest Players: Jeff Clark/SportsChrome (Lott); Jeff Glidden/AP (Favre); Heinz Kluetmeier (Payton); NFL/WireImage (Otto); Steve Hamm/AP (Smith); Walter Iooss Jr. (Greene, Youngblood); Allen Kee/WireImage (Matthews); Tony Tomsic (Lambert); Brian Garfinkel/Icon SMI (Runyan)
Hairstyles: Courtesy of Head and Shoulders (Polamalu); Joe Kohen/Getty Images for Audi of America (Brady); Michael J. Lebrecht II/1Deuce3 Photography (Ochocinco); Ron Chenoy/US Presswire (Tebow); Brian Bahr/Getty Images (Moss); Tim DeFrisco/Getty Images (Bosworth); Jed Jacobsohn/Getty Images (Peko); Gene Lower/Getty Images (Fitzgerald); John Bazemore/AP (Matthews); Al Tielemans (McNabb)
Running Backs: Walter Iooss Jr. (Brown, Dorsett); John Biever (Payton); Ronald Martinez/Getty Images (Smith); Chuck Solomon (Sanders); Vernon Biever/WireImage (Sayers); John Iacono (Campbell); John G. Mabanglo/AFP/Getty Images (Faulk); Jon Soohoo/Getty Images (Dickerson); John W. McDonough (Tomlinson)
Trick Plays: Bob Rosato (Titans, Ward); John Iacono (Dolphins); Jamie Squire/Getty Images (Pathon); Rob Tringali/Sports-Chrome (Brady); Justin Lane/EPA (Hester); The Times-Picayune/Landov (Carlson)
Other Sports: William R. Smith (Jackson); Syracuse University (Brown); Bettmann/Corbis (Thorpe); Al Tielemans (Sanders); Jerry Cooke (Hayes); Corbis (Graham); David Madison (Elway); Heinz Kluetmeier (Gault); John Biever (Peppers); Jonathan Daniel (Jordan)
Stadiums: Ronald Martinez/Getty Images (Cowboys Stadium); Scott Boehm/Getty Images (Soldier Field, Lambeau Field, Invesco Field, Lucas Oil Stadium, Ford Field); Jerry Driendl/Getty Images (Heinz Field); Kirby Lee/Getty Images (Qwest Field); David Drapkin/Getty Images (Arrowhead Stadium); Rick Stewart/Getty Images (Ralph Wilson Stadium)
Colorful Personalities: Heinz Kluetmeier (Sanders); Tony Triolo (Rossovich); Allen Kee/Getty Images (Randle); Dan Farrell/The New York Daily News/Getty Images (Namath); Gary Fitzgerald (Portis, 3); Paul Natkin/WireImage (McMahon); © Columbia Pictures/Everett Collection (Bosworth); Robert Beck (Sherman); Adam Larkey/ABC/AP (Ochocinco); Steve Morton/AP (Owens)
Sack Masters: Tony Tomsic (Jones); Allen Kee/Getty Images (White); Bill Frakes (Smith); John Biever (Taylor, Thomas); Jim McIsaac/Getty Images (Watt); Hy Peskin (Marchetti); Jeff Zelevansky/Getty Images (Ware); NFL/AP (Atkins); John Iacono (Strahan)
Accessories: Peter Read Miller (Tomlinson, McCaffrey); Ronald C. Modra (McMahon, Dickerson); Walter Iooss Jr. (shoes); David Liam Kyle (Cox); Simon Bruty (gloves); Al Tielemans (Sanders); Annmarie Avila (Sharpie); John Biever (Karlis)
Draft Busts: Al Messerschmidt/Wire Image (Leaf); David Bergman (Russell); Paul Warner/AP (Rogers); Suzanne Plunkett/AP (Couch); Ezra Shaw/Getty Images (Smith); Vernon Biever/WireImage (Mandarich); Mark Phillips/AFP/Getty Images (Carter); Scott Applewhite/AP (Shuler); NFL/WireImage (Thomas); Don Larson/Getty Images (Emtman)
Comebacks: John Biever (Bills–Oilers); Robert Beck (49ers–Saints); Scott Audette/AP (Colts–Bucs); Ray Stubblebine/Reuters (Jets–Dolphins); Rob Carr/Getty Images (Colts–Chiefs); Andy Lyons/Getty Images (Browns–Titans)
Quotes: Walter Iooss Jr. (Namath); John W. McDonough (Jackson); Mickey Pfleger (Rice); NFL/WireImage.com (Plank); Manny Rubio/WireImage.com (Perry); Albert Dickson/TSN/Icon SMI (Shula); Simon Bruty (Lewis); Peter Brouillet/WireImage.com (Hilgenberg); John Biever (Manning); Neil Leifer (Lombardi)
Fans: David E. Klutho (Bears, Chiefs); Bob Rosato (Steelers, Saints); John Biever (Packers); David Liam Kyle (Browns); V.J. Lovero (Raiders); David Bergman (Redskins); Tom Dahlin (Vikings); Simon Bruty (Cowboys)
Credits Page: Al Tielemans

Pittsburgh Steelers wide receiver Santonio Holmes makes the game-winning catch in Super Bowl XLIII.